Pictorial History of the
AUTOMOBILE
GRAHAM ROBSON

GALLERY BOOKS
An imprint of W.H. Smith Publishers Inc.
112 Madison Avenue
New York, New York 10016

A Bison Book

Contents

Published by Gallery Books
A Division of W H Smith Publishers Inc.
112 Madison Avenue
New York, New York 10016

Produced by
Bison Books Corp.
15 Sherwood Place
Greenwich, CT 06830

ISBN 0-8317-6893-2   Printed in Hong Kong

1 2 3 4 5 6 7 8 9 10

INTRODUCTION

A complete history of the automobile, and the world it has created, would fill many volumes. This book can only offer a taste of the fascinating cars, the outstanding personalities and the technical and social developments which have been prominent in the first 100 years of the industry. Without ignoring any major aspects of automobile history, I have tried to highlight the changes and innovations which have shaped its growth over the years. The pace of change has certainly been extraordinary — it is still staggering to realize that man could travel no faster than the speed of the galloping horse in the early 1800s, that the first spindly automobiles were not built until the 1880s, and that mass-production as we know it did not arrive until the 1900s.

The book underlines the changes in the relative importance of various continents. At first, certainly, Europe was dominant, but by the 1920s the United States was making all the running. Only in the last decade or so has Japan rushed through to challenge the American lead.

What will happen in the twenty-first century? I would be foolish to make any such forecast. Perhaps, in 20 years time, another edition may be needed.

GRAHAM ROBSON
Spring 1987

LEFT: *One of the world's most famous sports cars is the Chevrolet Corvette — this is a 1966 model.*

Page 1: Jaguar's legendary E-Type; Pages 2-3: The distinctive lines of a Duesenberg; Pages 4-5: Chevrolet's Corvette — the 1983 model.

The Victorian World on Wheels

Horses, Stage-Coaches, and Trains

AFTER more than 100 years of the automobile, it is now nearly impossible for us to visualize a world without cars, trucks or buses. In almost every way, the internal combustion engine has transformed the world in which we live. Before engines gave us the power to travel at unprecedented speeds, far beyond the reach of our own puny efforts, the world was huge; now it seems to have shrunk.

Although the world was already on wheels before the 1880s, life moved at a considerably slower pace. Before the arrival of railways there had been few innovations in transportation.

In the Stone Age, or perhaps somewhat later, *homo sapiens* learned how to tame oxen, horses and mules; he got up on their backs, rested his feet, and found that he could get around much easier than before. A little later, but still in ancient history – and who knows where it happened, or who did it – some genius invented the wheel. This allowed him or her to make carts to be dragged by tame beasts, and to be carried around in some style.

All this, of course, happened a long time before the birth of Christ, yet no radical improvements were then made to transportation systems for at least the next 2000 years. If anyone born in the Saxon era could have been carried forward to the first Elizabethan age, or even to the elegant Georgian times of the eighteenth century, he might have been surprised by the customs, the dress and some other aspects of living, but he would surely not have been surprised by the way people got about.

Quite simply, this was because man's only speedy means of transportation on land was the horse, while on the sea he still had to rely on ships which were propelled by the wind or by oars.

In the late eighteenth century, the freedom to move around was only available to those with money. The upper classes had their country estates and their town houses, traveling between the two by horse-drawn carriages of various sizes, but all of great opulence. A 60-mile journey from Blenheim Palace, near Oxford, to London, would take the Duke of Marlborough's carriage a day, and would involve several changes of horses along the way.

When the first explorers began to cross the North American continent they too used the same form of trans-

BELOW: *Until the 19th century, man could only get around at the speed of the galloping horse. But horses, like people, get tired, so long journeys took several days to complete.*

port that had been in use there for many years – namely the horse. And indeed it was the horse that led the railway across America; wherever civilization went, it was the horse that showed the way.

For those without their own horses, there was, of course, the stage-coach or mail service, but many of these journeys were made overnight, the fares were high unless one elected to ride outside, on top of the coach, and services were few and far between.

The roads, of course, were poor. The Romans had built many fine arteries all over Europe, but after their Empire collapsed, little further improvement was made to the road system. In Georgian times the roads, such as they were, had appalling surfaces that often became impassable in winter. On the American continent, roads simply didn't exist.

Then came the Industrial Revolution and the great surge forward in technology on so many fronts. At a time when James Watt's steam engine brought cheap power to many large businesses, engineers like Telford found ways of making road surfaces more stable. By the early nineteenth century, a densely populated country like Britain was served by a complex network of stage-coaches which used the newly surfaced roads to their utmost, and relied on a dense infrastructure of coaching inns, changes of horses in a matter of minutes and ruthless driving to increase their speeds.

Even so, London to Brighton in five hours, or London to York in 20 hours (both representing a 10mph average speed), was merely creditable, not remarkable. It still did not bring any country's provinces within easy or casual reach of its

BELOW: *The stage coach was the first type of 'mass transportation.' Cheapest seats were out on top.*

RIGHT: *As with trains, there were 'slow' coaches, or 'express' coaches. This was slow – 50 miles per day.*

YORK Four Days Stage-Coach.

Begins on Friday the 12th of April. 1706.

ALL that are desirous to pass from *London* to *York*, or from *York* to *London*, or any other Place on that Road; Let them Repair to the *Black Swan* in *Holbourn* in *London*, and to the *Black Swan* in *Coney street* in *York*.

At both which Places, they may be received in a Stage Coach every *Monday, Wednesday* and *Friday*, which performs the whole Journey in Four Days, (if God permits,) And sets forth at Five in the Morning.

And returns from *York* to *Stamford* in two days, and from *Stamford* by *Huntington* to *London* in two days more. And the like Stages on their return.

Allowing each Passenger 14ℓ, weight, and all above 3d a Pound.

Performed By { Benjamin Kingman, Henry Harrison, Walter Baynes.

Also this gives Notice that Newcastle Stage Coach, sets out from York, every Monday, and Friday, and from Newcastle every Monday and Friday.

Rec.d in p.t os.00. o of Mr. Bodingfeld for 5 for Monday the 3 of June 1706.

ABOVE: *This was the car's true ancestor – the carriage and pair. But horses had to be fuelled, even when at rest . . .*

RIGHT: *By the 1840s a railway network had spread across most of England, connecting the major towns and cities*

capital. Small wonder, therefore, that trips to foreign lands took weeks rather than hours, and that most people still stayed put.

The 'speed barrier' in those days was the speed of the horse – 20 mph over very short distances, 10-15 mph over longer ones – and there seemed to be no way of improving on this.

Then, in the nineteenth century, Britain's enterprising engineers married several inventions together – steam boilers, wheels and tramways. The result was the railway engine. By the middle of the century, railways linked many capitals with the provinces, and well before the end of the Victorian era every important town was connected to a railway. The coming of the railroad joined America for the first time into a single country; coast-to-coast travel became a reality although still something of an ordeal.

At a stroke, the speed of travel rose sharply. By mid-century it was usual for the crack express trains to complete up to 60 miles in an hour, and if the tracks were specially cleared and loads were lightened considerably, they could do even better.

Even so, for *individual* travel, even the wealthy could still make no progress. To return to our example of the Duke of Marlborough, he might be able to journey from Oxford to London's Paddington station by train in about 90 minutes, but this was only by traveling in a group with other people. In order to travel alone and make the same journey, he still had to rely on his horses.

The world, in other words, was still waiting for the horseless carriage.

A Horseless Carriage

Awaiting the Gasoline Engine

ABOVE: *Was this the world's first horseless carriage? This was the Frenchman Cugnot's steam-powered carriage of 1769. It was to prove unsuccessful.*

HORSE-DRAWN carriages look splendid these days — which is fine because we don't have to rely on them for everyday transport. Apart from having severely limited speed and endurance, horses had several other drawbacks. They were very expensive to run (you cannot 'switch off' an animal when it is not being used — it has to be fed, watered, sheltered and groomed at all times); they produced copious and distressing exhaust emissions; and their manure positively encouraged the growth and the spreading of diseases. All the romantic memories that horse-drawn traffic evokes tend to block out unpleasant details such as manure-heaped roadways and unhygenic city streets — problems that were growing in intensity during the course of the nineteenth century.

To replace a horse, alternative power was needed. It is a credit to the universal use to which horses were put that all machines designed to replace them had their abilities measured in — horsepower! However, it was one thing to design stationary machines or mobile ones that could be large and heavy, but it was quite another to replace the horse-drawn carriage.

In the seventeenth century, inventors wondered if they could use some sort of clockwork power, but this was clearly not an answer. In the eighteenth century, after the steam engine made its name in heavy industry, there were thoughts of harnessing a small steam engine to the carriage. The problem was that one could not 'scale down' steam engines to be reasonably light and efficient. Cugnot's *fardier*, briefly tried in Paris at the time, proved how difficult it was. Coal and water had to be carried on board, and both were bulky and heavy.

It was agreed that the steam engine's principle and linkage — converting pressure on a reciprocating piston into rotary motion at an output shaft — was right for the hoped-for horseless carriage. Thoughts then turned to the idea of exploding gases inside engines by an electric spark, perhaps using coal gas, but storage of fuel once again proved to be impossible.

It was, however, the further development of a gas engine, invented by the Belgian, Etienne Lenoir, which heralded the breakthrough. Lenoir's original engine of 1859 was large, heavy and inefficient, but a much modified unit, produced in 1863, held more promise.

By that time a new and magical mineral, crude oil, had been discovered under the earth's surface, and a refined derivative of it, with the name 'petrol' patented by Carless, Capel and Leonard, was seen to provide a good alternative to coal gas in Lenoir's engine. Petrol, or gasoline, was a substance that could be stored safely in cans or in a tank near the engine and, weight for weight, it was a much more efficient fuel than gas or coal.

The best gas-powered Lenoir horseless carriage managed to complete a six-mile journey in three hours (with innumerable breakdowns) in 1863. This was clearly not good enough, and the project was abandoned. At this point, however, Nikolaus August Otto (of the German engineering company Gasmotorenfabrik Deutz) invented the now-familiar 'four stroke' engine, which took the Lenoir idea several stages further, used gasoline as its easy-to-carry fuel, and allowed a unit to be made much smaller than hitherto. The four-stroke cycle (induction, compression, explosion, exhaust) was patented in 1876. This was the real breakthrough that the horseless carriage needed.

Perhaps the importance of this invention was not realized at the time, for the idea of steam traction was still alive and well — indeed, the last series-production steam car, the Franklin, would not be built until 1934 — but from the late 1870s several resourceful designers began to look on engines using the 'Otto' cycle as the answer to their needs. Even so, it would be another decade before the world's first viable horseless carriage took to the roads.

BELOW: *Steam power was more suitable for large vehicles. The 'Enterprise' omnibus first ran in 1833.*

RIGHT: *The Marquis de Dion built this steam-powered tricycle in 1887, but it was not a success.*

The Dawn of Motoring

Otto, Daimler, and Benz

WHENEVER the birth of the automobile is discussed, three names stand out; all of them, Nikolaus Otto, Gottlieb Daimler and Karl Benz, were German. It was Nikolaus Otto's engine principle that made the horseless carriage practical, while it was Benz and Daimler, working independently, who first married this engine to carriages that could be driven. No matter what other chauvinistic nations – and historians – might tell you, the automobile as we know it was invented in Germany.

Otto first worked with another engineer, Eugen Langen, to develop a free-piston engine, then reorganized their company as Gasmotorenfabrik Deutz, and employed a 38-year-old engineer called Gottlieb Daimler as factory manager. It was Daimler, working sometimes with Otto and at other times on his own, who developed the four-stroke cycle to something approaching practicality. This principle was patented, but the patent was later overthrown when it was discovered that a French scientist (Beau de Rochas) had earlier postulated the theory, on paper, although he had never built an engine to prove his point.

Even at the beginning of the 1880s, when the existence of Otto's engine principle was becoming known in Germany, and when petroleum (a by-product of a process used to refine lamp oil from crude, and hitherto considered useless) was already freely available, there was still no rush to produce a viable horseless carriage.

By that time, however, Karl Benz (born near Karlsruhe in 1844) had founded Benz und Ritter (later reformed as Gasmotorenfabrik), had started building two-stroke gas engines, and was struggling to make a living. Breaking free of this, he then founded Benz und Cie and, in the winter of 1883-84 began developing his own engineering ideas, which included gasoline-powered engines.

Benz did not realize that he had a rival in Gottlieb Daimler, who had left Gasmotorenfabrik Deutz to set up shop in Bad Cannstatt (near Stuttgart) with Wilhelm Maybach, also to develop high-speed gasoline-powered engines. The two inventors went ahead in isolation, and in ignorance of each other's intentions, for the next couple of years.

As it happened, they produced their first machines at about the same time, both put them falteringly on trial at the same time, and by 1886 both had achieved some sort of reliability from their inventions. Great minds, however, did not

ABOVE RIGHT: *The four-stroke Otto engine made motor cars practical. This was the one-cylinder Daimler of 1885.*

RIGHT: *Karl Benz produced the first petrol-engined tricycie in 1885-86, which started the motoring boom.*

LEFT: *The original trend-setting Benz had an engine under the seats, with a massive, exposed flywheel.*

RIGHT: *Both Daimler's and Benz's projects vie for the title of the 'World's First Car.' This was the Benz tricycle of 1885-86, built in Mannheim.*

BELOW: *In 1885, before Gottlieb Daimler built his first car, he produced the world's first motorcycle, with a wooden frame, and single-cylinder engine.*

think alike, for Benz's first machine was a tricycle, with two driven rear wheels, while Daimler's first engine-powered device was in fact a motorcycle, his first horseless carriage a four-wheeler.

The building of the Benz tricycle began in 1885, its first unsuccessful trial run was apparently in October of that year, and a patent relating to its design was granted in January 1886. Yet it was not until later in 1886 that it began to run properly, or to be seen around the streets of Mannheim. Its first motor show was the Paris Exhibition of 1887.

The Benz tricycle had a single-cylinder, water-cooled horizontal engine mounted amidships in the frail-looking tricycle (under the bench seat). Drive to the rear wheels was by belt, chain and a differential gear, and from a 1.0-liter capacity it produced about 0.8hp. Later a 1.7-liter 1.5hp engine was substituted, to give the little machine a viable performance.

Benz was not yet ready to put his machine on sale, even though his resourceful wife proved its reliability by taking her two teenage children for a long drive in one of the prototypes, from Mannheim to Pforzheim (62 miles) and back in 1888.

Meanwhile, in 1885 Daimler built his pioneering bicycle, which had wooden wheels and a 0.5hp 264cc single-cylinder engine. This, however, was only a try-out for the new technology, for with a certain amount of logic Daimler then decided to graft an engine into a carriage normally pulled by horses. Accordingly, he went to a local coachbuilder, bought the carriage, discarded the shafts and designed a vertical steering column instead – and set about installing an engine.

As in the Benz tricycle, the engine was mounted amidships, but not in so elegant a fashion. On the first car the 1.1hp 462cc single-cylinder engine was ahead of the line of the rear wheels, poking up through the floor of the rear passenger compartment. The Daimler also had a crude type of differential (using slipping leather discs to match the requirements of outer and inner rear wheels on corners), with final drive to the rear wheels by belts, pulleys and gears.

It was, of course, the world's first *four*-wheeler horseless carriage. Completed in 1886, it was soon to be seen journeying between Cannstatt and Unterturkheim, the latter village later to become very important to the story of the Daimler and Daimler-Benz companies.

Daimler's second car, the two-seater Stahlrad, was more logically thought out than the first, for the engine was mounted lower, under the seat and had a narrow-angle V-twin layout. Not only that, it had a four-speed transmission with a specially designed steel chassis frame.

The horseless carriage – or shall we start to call it the car? – was now a reality, but there was still a long way to go before commercial sales could begin.

98071

Cars go on Sale

Germany and France take the lead

WHEN Benz and Daimler built the world's first gasoline-powered automobiles in Germany, the law made it almost impossible for them to be driven properly. In Baden province, where the Benz was produced, the speed limit in towns was 4mph, in the country 8mph. In some parts of Germany it was quite illegal for such machines to be used on the public highway at all.

Nevertheless, some progress was made. Daimler supplied a machine for taxicab use at Stuttgart station in 1888, and a fire engine soon followed. In 1887 Daimler negotiated the French manufacturing rights to Edouard Sarazin (a Belgian), who turned to the small company of Panhard et Levassor to make the engines for him. Benz, on the other hand, was not yet ready to start selling in Germany, the first concession and deliveries going to Emile Roger's business in Paris.

The problem was, of course, that without a demand from customers, there could be no industry, and without an industry there could be no deliveries to customers. Catch 22? Yes – except that the phrase had yet to be invented. . .

It was in France that the motoring craze first began to spread, encouraged by the *Machines et Moteurs* and *Charronage* displays at the 1889 World's Fair in Paris. During the six months that this great exhibition was open, both Benz and Daimler engines were on show. Daimler exhibited his latest 1.6hp V-twin engined car and Emile Roger showed the most modern Benz tricycle.

Things now started to move fast. René Panhard and Emile Levassor began manufacturing Daimler engines, supplying three early examples to another French manufacturer, Armand Peugeot, and both of them decided to start building cars. By the early 1890s, therefore, a fledgling industry was beginning to take shape.

Benz, the tricycle pioneer, concentrated on selling stationary engines for a time, sold a few tricycles through Emile Roger in France, and did not build his first four-wheeler, the Viktoria, until 1893. This was a great success, with 45 built and sold in the first year, and (along with the smaller-engined Velo derivative) no fewer than 572 machines were built in 1899. At that moment, Benz was dominant in the new automobile industry.

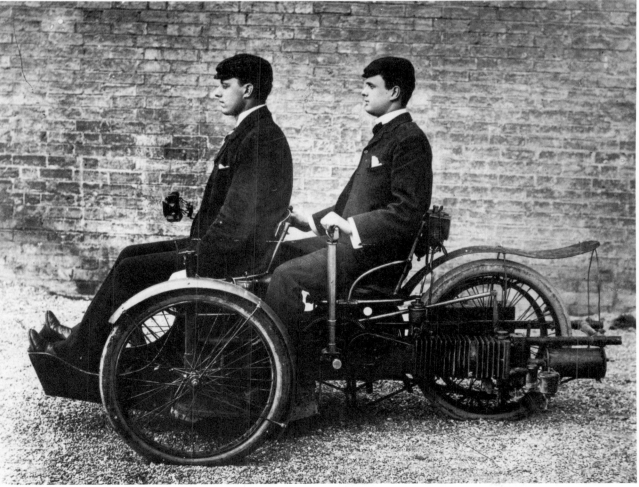

ABOVE RIGHT:*This belt-driven Daimler of 1892 had a twin-cylinder engine under the body; its styling is clearly derived from that of a horse-drawn carriage. With a 2.5hp engine this car could achieve 12mph.*

RIGHT: *It took time for motoring pioneers to agree on the ideal layout for a car. Here is the Hon. CS Rolls 'driving' his 1897 Leon Bollée tricycle, with the passenger ahead of him.*

LEFT: *Daimler's first car was obviously a 'horseless carriage', with the single-cylinder engine mounted amidships ahead of the rear seat, and with a vertical steering column.*

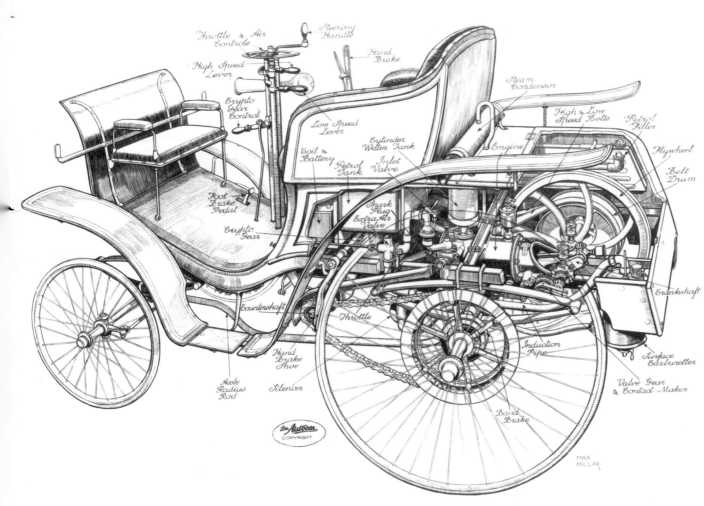

ABOVE: *Lanchester was one of the successful British pioneers, utilising advanced technical features. This car dates from 1901.*

LEFT: *The anatomy of early motor cars laid bare – this is an 1897 Benz, showing the rear-mounted engine, and chain drive system.*

OPPOSITE ABOVE: *De Dion of France soon started building cars in numbers – this was a 1902 Motorette model.*

OPPOSITE: *Panhard's contribution to motoring was to locate the engine up front with rear-wheel-drive – a 1900 model.*

All the flavor of Edwardian motoring – British tourists in France in 1904, using a 24hp Fiat.

Daimler progress was held back by a dispute between Daimler and Maybach on one side and their co-directors on the other. It all turned sour: Daimler and Maybach set up shop on their own for a time and did not make their peace again until 1895. By this time, however, Daimler patents were not only licensed in mainland Europe, but also in the British Empire. Frederick Simms acquired them at first, but he did not proceed seriously with manufacturing plans. Instead, he sold out to a syndicate headed by Harry Lawson, who started production in Coventry in 1896.

Panhard-Levassor's first-ever car was built at the end of 1890 and became reliable in 1891 (when Panhard completed a Paris-Normandy trip of 140 miles in two days). This, however, was a mid-engined device, and it was Emile Levassor's decision to design a completely different car, with an engine at the front and drive to the rear wheels, which really set the world's automobile industry on the right path. The *système Panhard*, as it became known, placed its transmission behind the engine, and had final drive by twin side chains. It was at once practical, economical and easy to build. From late 1891, Panhards of this type went on sale, and the company did not look back. (There was nothing new about this layout, by the way, which had first been seen on Bollée's La Mancelle steam vehicle of 1878.)

Peugeot's first horseless carriage prototype had been a Ser-pollet-engined steam-powered device, also shown at the World's Fair in 1889, but it was during that fair that Armand Peugeot decided to use Panhard-built, Daimler-licensed gasoline engines. The first such Peugeot, built in 1890, had a bicycle-type tubular steel frame and was really a refined version of the mid-engined Daimler Stahlrad design, although fitted with transverse leaf-spring front suspension. The first hand-built Peugeots were delivered in 1891 and sales in numbers began soon afterwards.

At this point in history, the world's automobile industry consisted of just four manufacturers – Benz, Daimler, Panhard-Levassor and Peugeot – with its center of gravity still in the German engines of Benz and Daimler. Other countries – the United States, Britain and Italy among them – were waiting in the wings, but for the moment the glory belonged to France and, above all, Germany.

But not for long. The industrial might of the United States was about to join in.

Pioneers in the New World

America gets in on the act

IN the 1880s and 1890s, the world was still a large place, so it took a little time for the fame of Benz and Daimler to float across the Atlantic to the United States. However, once this young, vigorous and technically ambitious nation got involved in the development of cars, progress was extremely rapid.

The very first American motor vehicle seems to have been the steam-powered Schank tricycle, which was shown at the Ohio State Fair in 1886. This was quite impractical (the engine was reputed to have been as 'large as a kitchen stove'), but at least it inspired a cycle manufacturer called Charles Duryea to start experiments of his own.

By 1891 the New York piano-maker William Steinway had secured American patent rights from Gottlieb Daimler, but he took time to set up a factory on Long Island, and then mainly made stationary and marine engines. The first successful American car was a three-wheeler designed by John W Lambert of Ohio City, which was demonstrated early in 1891, though never developed. In the same year Henry and Philip Nadig of Allentown, Pennsylvania, produced a single-cylinder four-wheeler, two years later substituted a two-cylinder engine, and ran the car until 1903.

Neither of these cars, however, went into production. The honor of being America's first domestically designed production car went to the Duryea of 1895. The first Duryea prototype of 1893, which was built at Springfield, Massachusetts, was really a converted horse buggy with a single-cylinder engine, had friction drive and was a failure. The

TOP: *North America's first production car was the Duryea, built in Springfield from 1895. This very early example (dating from 1896) has tiller steering and is about as simple as a car can be.*

LEFT: *This 1902 Cadillac helped found the reputation of one of the world's great marques. In the next few years the Cadillac got bigger, faster, and more grand.*

definitive production car of 1895 had a 1¾ hp twin-cylinder engine with a three-speed transmission and an unsprung rear axle. It was much more successful and sales began at once.

At this point a New York solicitor, George Baldwin Selden, published his original patent application of 1879 (why had it taken him 16 years to get round to it?), which defined a 'reliable road locomotive' with an engine 'of the compression type' in rather vague terms. Although he had not actually built a prototype to prove his principle, on these grounds he claimed that all gasoline-driven vehicles developed since then infringed his patents, and that according to United States law these patents would hold for the next 17 years. He did not immediately try to enforce these claims. Most nascent United States car-makers, in fact, did not even know that they might be transgressing a patent.

The 'Selden Patent' only became public knowledge, and was enforced, after a company which became the Electric Vehicle Company (EVC) took up the patents, and in 1902 began to enforce a royalty through the newly formed Association of Licensed Automobile Manufacturers (ALAM). If the

stubborn Henry Ford had not decided to challenge this patent, Selden, the EVC and the ALAM might all have been receiving a fat income for life. As it was, Ford fought the patent through court after court, finally winning his case in 1911.

Before the end of the 1890s, however, more and more American car companies had been founded, and in 1899 it was estimated that 57 companies employed 2241 people. Five years later, as the popularity of the automobile mushroomed, there were 178 companies and more then 12,000 workers. About 50 American-built cars existed by 1900, but within a year there were 4192 on the still-awful roads, and by 1905 this figure had rocketed to 24,250. Consider these famous names:

Ransom Olds began playing around with steam and electric cars, saying that he 'couldn't stand the smell of horses,' but his first gasoline-driven car was the legendary Curved Dash Oldsmobile, which went on sale in 1901. This stubby little creation had a water-cooled engine lying amidships under the floor and longitudinal leaf springs connecting front and rear axles. By 1905, 36 cars a day were being

OPPOSITE: *At its height, Packard was one of the USA's most important auto makers, although it all started modestly, with models like this 1900 example.*

RIGHT: *One of America's memorable early cars, the famous 'curved dash' Oldsmobile.*

BELOW: *By 1908 Packard had become larger and more grand; already this was one of the more patrician American makes.*

BELOW: *By 1910 American cars were taking on a distinctive style – this being an Oldsmobile.*

BOTTOM *A famous, if not a significant Ford: an 1896 Quadricycle, with Henry at the wheel.*

produced at the Lansing, Michigan, factory. Oldsmobile became a member of the General Motors Corporation a few years later.

Alexander Winton was a Cleveland bicycle-maker who built his first experimental car in 1897 and started selling two-cylinder cars in 1898. Among the earliest Winton customers were the Packard brothers, and it is said that Winton's attitude to complaints led to the Packards setting up their own business.

JW and WD Packard set up shop at Warren, Ohio, in 1899, and their first car was a single-cylinder 12hp model. This was soon supplanted by faster and more powerful versions, and in 1903 one of the latest cars was driven from San Francisco to New York in 61 days. Packard moved to Detroit in 1903 and remained an independent concern until 1954.

I should also mention bathtub-maker David Buick's first car of 1903, the original Cadillac of 1903, and the Rambler, built by the Jefferys family from 1902. Plus, of course, Ford.

Ford's impact on the American way of life was so enormous that a separate section is devoted to the company's growth (*see* page 51).

FIRST · CAR

The Best Car in the World

Rolls-Royce or Cadillac?

TOP: *Only a marque like Cadillac, so sure of its reputation, would call this interesting 1910 model a 'Runabout.'*

ABOVE: *The Alpine Eagle version of the Rolls-Royce 40/50hp model, participating in a 1914 alpine trial.*

THERE are some conundrums that defy analysis. Facts are facts and can be displayed, but opinions can only be justified by emotion and passion. Here is a perennial riddle — what is, or was, the Best Car in the World?

British enthusiasts have no doubt, but Germans would disagree. As for the Americans — one of the easiest ways to start an argument with them is to suggest that Rolls-Royce have *always* built the best cars in the world, and that Cadillac, Lincoln or Duesenberg do not figure.

Even in the early 1900s, when the art and science of building cars was developing so precariously, a few types of car stood out from the common herd. By 1910 the well-to-do knew where they should be buying their cars. By 1920 the list was well established, and nothing that has happened since 1930 has changed that.

In Britain, the best of the best was undoubtedly Rolls-Royce. In Germany it was Mercedes. In the United States it was Cadillac. If Mercedes (later Mercedes-Benz) had not then gone for the sporting market instead of the custom of the 'carriage trade', they might always have been rivals for the crown; in the event, it was not until the 1960s that they came back with a real challenger.

Rolls-Royce, in fact, was born out of Henry Royce's dissatisfaction with a French Decauville which he ran for a short time. The Manchester-based electrical engineer who designed and developed better cars, joined up in a marketing arrangement with the Hon. Charles Rolls, and began to evolve the Rolls-Royce marque. Royce was happy to let high-class coachbuilders produce bodywork for these cars; the Manchester and (later) the Derby factories only produced Rolls-Royce rolling chassis.

The first of the truly great Rolls-Royces was the 40/50hp model (also colloquially known as the 'Silver Ghost'), an expensive and magnificently detailed 7.0-liter (later 7.4-liter) six-cylinder machine whose basic design was to run through until 1925. The 'Ghost' nickname, incidentally, was applied after the quietness and refinement of the splendid engine became apparent.

For many years, a Rolls-Royce chassis was designed and built almost without regard to cost. Royce the perfectionist knew only one way to design anything – the best way – and if this was expensive it had to be accepted. For that reason it always took a long time for the latest technical trends to be accepted – just in case the trend was only a craze – and the well-proven solution to a problem was always preferred to the latest gimmick.

On the other hand, Royce and his successors were always happy to go out and buy the rights to a new component (or copy a good idea!) if it seemed suitable for Rolls-Royce cars. In the 1920s the Hispano-Suiza mechanical brake servo was used, while in the 1930s the new-fangled General Motors synchromesh soon put in an appearance. Later in the decade, the company's first independent front suspension layout was apparently based on that used by the American Packard concern.

LEFT: *Full pre-war magnificence expressed in this 1912 Rolls-Royce 40/50hp model.*

BELOW: *The Rolls-Royce 'Alpine Eagle' of 1913, a real sports car.*

OPPOSITE: *A USA-built Springfield Rolls-Royce of 1926.*

OPPOSITE BELOW: *So typical of early 1920s American styling – the 1920 Cadillac 59 Victoria.*

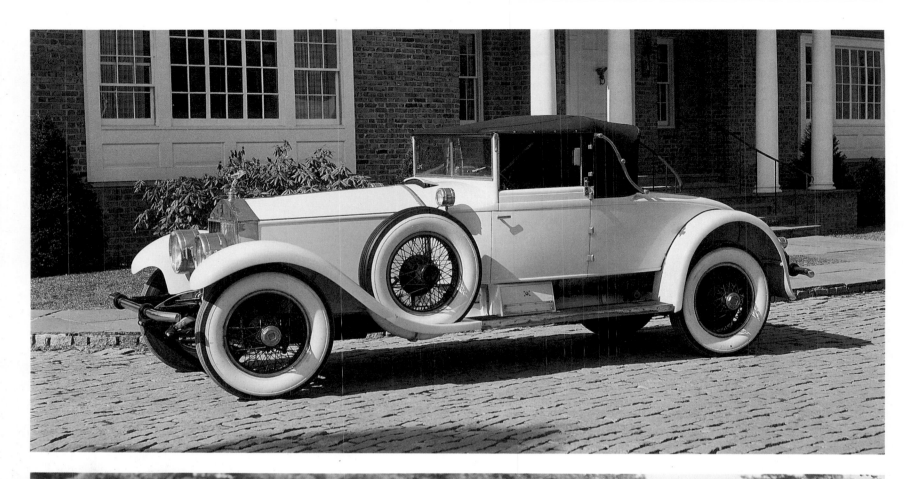

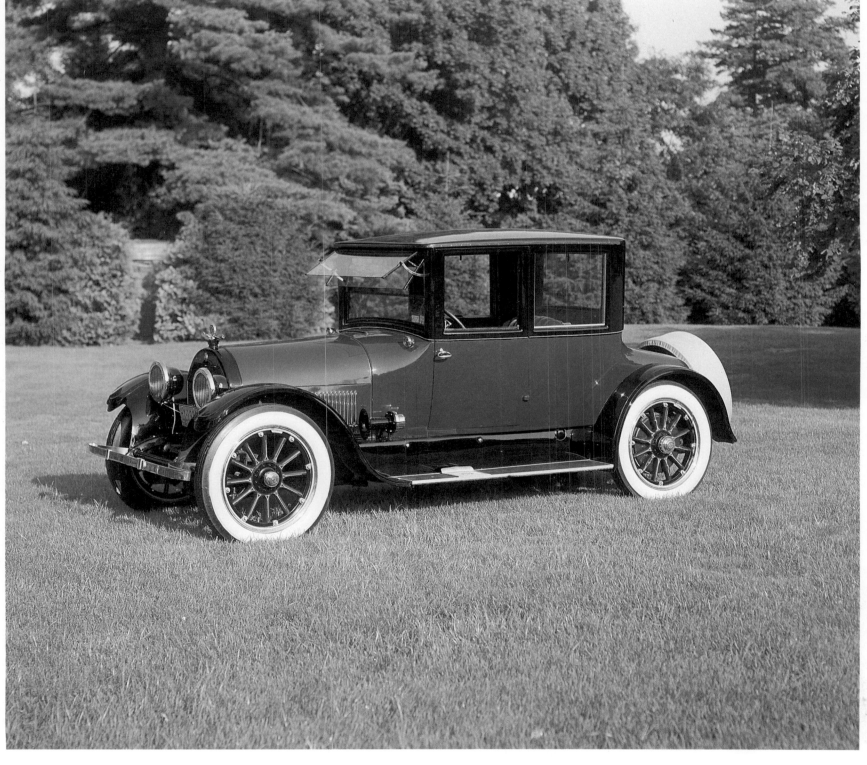

To supplement the 40/50hp, Rolls-Royce produced the 3.1-liter 20hp model from 1922, and in 1925 the original 40/50hp was displaced by the 7.7-liter engined New Phantom (also known as Phantom I). For the next 10 years both types were gradually improved – 20hp becoming 20/25, then 25/30, and finally Wraith, New Phantom becoming Phantom II – until, in 1935, came the most complex Rolls-Royce so far, the 7.3-liter engined V12 Phantom III. By 1939, however, much of the Rolls-Royce business was concentrated on the building of aircraft engines (including the magnificent V12 Merlin unit), and cars were almost an irrelevance.

From 1921 to 1931, the 40/50hp and later the New Phantom chassis were also manufactured in the United States, at Springfield, Massachusetts, and were graced with sumptuous American-built coachwork. The effects of the Depression finally put paid to what was never a profitable venture.

The name 'Cadillac' came from the French army officer, Antoine de la Mothe Cadillac, who founded the city of Detroit in 1701. It was William Murphy who adopted this name when setting up his new car company, in Detroit, in 1902. He got Henry M Leland to design his new car for him. Cadillac's motto : 'Craftsmanship a creed, accuracy a law,' stems from those early days and, in spite of the styling excesses committed in its name in later years, it was usually adhered to.

The first Cadillac was a single-cylinder four-seater tourer, and it was the Model K version of this design which added the name Cadillac to the automobile hall of fame. In Britain, to prove Cadillac's ideas about precision manufacture and interchangeability of parts, three cars were completely stripped out, the parts mixed up, then reassembled in no particular way, run for 500 miles at the Brooklands race track, and encountered no problems at all.

Cadillac's growing reputation led to the company being absorbed into the new General Motors combine in 1909, and it was under General Motors ownership that the first Cadillac V8 was introduced in 1915. During the 1920s, Cadillacs usually looked conventional (some say undistinguished), but always had impeccably engineered chassis. While Rolls-

FAR LEFT: *The Rolls-Royce 40/50hp, or 'Silver Ghost,' was built until the mid-1920s. This is one of the last, produced in 1925.*

LEFT: *If Rolls-Royce could have its Spirit of Ecstasy, so could Cadillac! This is the V16 radiator mascot of 1931.*

ABOVE: *Cadillac's most complex and expensive between-wars car was the V16 model, launched in 1930 and soon joined by a V12 version. Rolls-Royce did not match such enterprise until 1935.*

Royce were only building 1000 cars a year, Cadillac produced 47,420 in 1927.

Cadillac introduced the electric self-starter, the generator, even the high-tension electrical system named after its inventor, GM's 'Boss' Kettering. In 1928 there was not only a new V8 engine, but the world's first use of synchromesh transmission. Vacuum-boosted brakes were provided from 1932 and independent front suspension soon followed.

Cadillac's most startling innovations of the 1930s, however, were the 165hp 7.4-liter 45-degree V16 engine of 1930, which appeared at the beginning of the Depression, and the closely related V12 which followed it. From 1941, too, there was the world's first fully automatic transmission as an option. The adoption of the Cadillac motto 'Standard of the World,' is hardly a surprise.

But, which was the Best Car in the World? I leave you to argue it out.

Edwardian Magnificence

The Great Marques develop

BY the beginning of the 1900s, automobiles were no longer viewed as playthings or as a passing fancy. They were seen as a permanent and important new mode of transportation. The horse was still the most popular way of getting around in the 1890s, but by the 1910s it had been rendered almost obsolete.

The early 1900s was a time when many now-famous marques were founded or came to prominence. As the motoring habit spread, first all over Europe and soon into North America as well, car companies mushroomed. In 1890 there had only been four makes of car, but by 1900 there were 110. Ten years later, many of those marques had disappeared, but hundreds more had been designed, tested and put on sale.

All of the original pioneers – Benz, Daimler, Panhard-Levassor and Peugeot – went from strength to strength and retained their independence for many years to come. It was Daimler which made the next big leap forward. The Consul-General in Nice for the Austro-Hungarian Empire, Emil Jellinek, joined the Daimler board, persuaded them to build an entirely new type of car, and as the price of taking an agency to sell the first batch insisted that the new car should be called after his daughter – Mercedes. Thus it was that one of the world's great cars was born.

The 35hp Mercedes had an altogether more modern, lower and more integrated design than previous Daimlers. It was also faster and handled better, so everyone loved it. Before long, the old 'Daimler' name had disappeared completely, as a succession of new cars – 60hp, 90hp and 120hp monsters among them – was developed on Mercedes lines. At a stroke, it seemed, Jellinek had inspired the birth of the modern automobile, and his daughter's name was to become famous all over the world.

In Britain, the Daimler Motor Company soon shrugged off both the German design influence and the malign management of Harry Lawson's cronies, and began to develop a series of fine, fast cars. It was Daimler, more than any other European manufacturer, that popularized the use of the American Knight double-sleeve valve engine (quieter, but more complex, than the usual type of poppet-valve engine). Helped along by royal patronage (for the British royal family preferred Daimlers to Rolls-Royce cars at first), Daimler developed its 'cars for the gentry' image and was certainly one of the country's 'top' cars by 1914.

Napier, on the other hand, fought hard for the same status. It was already a precision-engineering firm before it hired SF Edge to distribute and publicize its new-fangled cars. Its best Edwardian cars were huge, powerful and beautifully made, so it was reasonable of the American Charles J

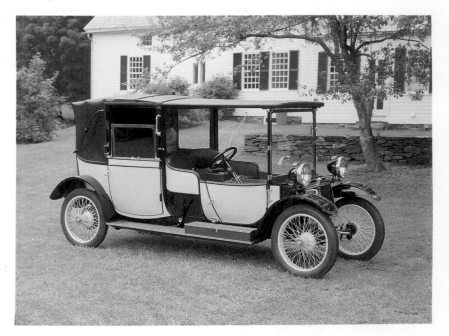

ABOVE: *A different styling quirk from Lanchester.*

BELOW: *The 40hp Delauney Belleville of 1908, was large, heavy, and very dignified.*

RIGHT: *By 1908 the French Delauney Belleville with circular-radiator was rightly thought to be one of the world's best-looking cars.*

Glidden to use Napiers for his world-encircling tours. Edge drove on to victory in the Gordon Bennett race of 1902, and in 1904 Napier put the world's first six-cylinder car on sale. It was a Napier that set 24-hour records at the newly opened Brooklands race track and a Napier that won the Tourist Trophy race in 1908. The Acton factory was building 11 different models by 1911, but in spite of magnificent styling (and that unmistakable 'water-tower' radiator filler cap), the marque could not quite match the upper-class cachet of a Rolls-Royce or a Daimler. In the meantime, the Métallurgique had been developed in Belgium, destined to become one of the most renowned sports cars of the era. The first Métallurgiques had German Daimler-style lines, but before long unique new cars, with twin- and four-cylinder engines, came along. From 1906 there was the splendid 100hp fast tourer, a year later the famous V-radiator style was adopted, and in the next two years the 40hp model and the famous 26hp were introduced. By 1914 the company was at the height of its reputation.

In Italy, Cesare Isotta and Vincenzo Fraschini started importing Renaults in 1899, built Renault-based cars called Isotta-Fraschinis in the next few years, and then began producing Italian designs from 1903. The original cars had Mercedes-type four-cylinder engines, the largest being a 7433cc 24hp model, and by 1907 there was the massive 11.3-liter Tipo C. By that time, Isotta was second only to Fiat in Italy, and after a short period of ownership by Lorraine-Dietrich

several ultra-sporting cars like the TM and KM models were introduced. Isotta-Fraschini cars were to become even more magnificent in the 1920s, when a series of fast and powerful eight-cylinder cars were produced.

Austro-Daimler, naturally enough, was an offshoot of the German Daimler company, with a factory in Wiener-Neustadt. In 1906 it became a separate company with the young Ferdinand Porsche as chief designer, and a series of smart, powerful and fast machines resulted. It was in motor sport, notably the Prince Henry Tour of 1910 and the Austrian Alpine of 1911, that the Austro-Daimler marque made its name. Porsche stayed with this famous company until he moved on to Daimler (later Daimler-Benz) in 1923.

Last, and by no means least, of my Edwardian 'Great Marques' was the Hispano-Suiza, a company whose name confirms that it had links with Spain, where the first cars were built, and Switzerland, which was the homeland of the company's chief designer Marc Birkigt. The original Hispanos were massive, beautifully built four-cylinder machines produced in Barcelona, and soon attracted Spanish royal patronage. The largest of all had 10.4-liter engines. Then came the Alfonso XIII model of 1912, which was a sports car.

At this stage, however, Hispano-Suiza became equally famous for its advanced and powerful aircraft engines, design features of which were to be found in the great Hispano-Suiza models announced in 1913, and in the legendary six-cylinder and V12 models of the 1920s and 1930s.

LEFT: *De Dietrich of France started building modest little cars in 1897, but in the early 1900s the company was best known for the large four-cylinder engined machines depicted here.*

BELOW: *The first British Daimlers were license-built German machines, but the company soon gained design independence. This was a 15hp two-seater built in 1910.*

BOTTOM: *From 1909 Cadillac became part of General Motors, but this 1911 model still has all the hallmarks of a hand-built car. Note – spare tire, but no spare wheel!*

Motoring for the Masses

The rise of Ford, and General Motors

FOR the first 20 years or so the automobile tended to be the rich man's plaything, built in small numbers by craftsmen in small factories, with the very minimum of mechanization and tooling. It was not until North American entrepreneurs got their teeth into the problem, realizing the potential of 'wheels for the world,' that the automobile began to reach the mass market.

Right from the start, Detroit emerged as the center of North America's automobile industry, though it was not until the late 1900s that the large companies began to appear. Until then, cars like Oldsmobile, Buick, and Ford were separately built, in larger quantities than those being produced in Europe at that time, but still not in the huge numbers that were to become standard.

For the Americans, motoring for the masses gradually evolved between 1900 and 1910, when two large concerns began to emerge — Ford and General Motors. Then, as now, they were the most important influences on any other car-maker in the country. The only difference between Detroit in the 1910s and 1920s and the Detroit of today is that Ford was then substantially larger than General Motors.

Henry Ford came from a farming family, but he gravitated to Detroit in the 1890s (before an automobile industry had been set up), was fascinated by engineering, and began working for the Edison Illuminating Company. For his own interest, Henry Ford built the Quadricycle prototype in 1896, but it was not until he set up the Detroit Automobile Company (DAC) that he began to sell cars to the public.

Like many such small firms, DAC failed, so the 38-year-old Ford had to start again, this time with the Henry Ford Company and, shortly, with the Ford Motor Co. Ltd in 1903. That family-owned company then set down roots, and grew and grew, until it became the biggest car-making complex in the world. The initial capitalization was $28,000 and the first cars cost $850. Success was swift, for within a year vast profits were being made and almost $100,000 was paid out in dividends.

The first production Ford was the Model A, but it was the Model T, announced in 1908, that really rocketed the company to worldwide fame. To make more and more of these cars, the massive Highland Park factory was built, assembly plants were opened in other countries, then after World War I the River Rouge 'greenfield' site was developed; that

OPPOSITE: *After building more than 15 million Model Ts, Ford produced the all-new, very different Model A in 1927.*

BELOW: *Buick was one of the founder members of the General Motors group. This car, a 10E model, was produced in 1909.*

ABOVE: A Model T Ford, one of the 15 million built between 1908 and 1927. This particular car dates from 1916, and at that stage the Model T still had no front wheel brakes. Model T styling changed only slowly over the years and the famous radiator style was always retained.

LEFT: Walter Chrysler, formerly of Buick and Willys, set up his own business in 1923, and soon had a fine reputation. Before long Chrysler was the third most important grouping in the USA. This was a 1927 Tourer.

OPPOSITE: Chrysler's first production car was the six-cylinder engined '70.' This is the Model B Phaeton of 1924.

factory is still the pivot of Ford's United States assembly today.

Along the way Henry Ford controlled his company and its thousands of workers in a very paternal way. He introduced the $5-day at a time when most Detroit car-makers paid $2, he refused to allow unions in his factories until the late 1930s, and he refused to see a Model T successor developed until 1927, when it was almost too late. That was the moment when General Motors took over market leadership, which they have never relinquished.

General Motors was founded in 1908 by the wheeler-dealing William C Durant, who had been in control of Buick since 1904. By 1907 Buick was selling 8800 cars a year, second only to Ford's total of 10,200, having come up from nothing five years earlier. One of its rivals was Cadillac, a company that had been building cars since 1903. Another competitor, Oldsmobile, was one of the United States' car-making pioneers with prototypes on the road in 1896. Its small 'curved-dash' model made it one of America's most notable car-making companies in the early 1900s. Durant master-minded a merger between Buick, Cadillac and Oldsmobile to form General Motors. Ford might also have been included, but the irascible Henry could not stomach such a deal.

At that stage, what is now General Motors' largest name-plate, the Chevrolet, had not even come into existence. In 1910, in a complex financial situation, GM's bankers ousted Durant from the chair, whereupon he went off with racing driver Louis Chevrolet and developed the new Chevrolet road car. Eventually Durant bought his way back into control of General Motors in 1915, but he did not add the Chevrolet marque to the group until 1918.

Other cars, such as Oakland, Sheridan and Scripps-Booth, were also manufactured under the General Motors umbrella, but the group remained a corporate shambles until Alfred P Sloan became executive vice-president in 1921. In the next years, Sloan transformed the agglomerate into a much more logical group, sales rose, costs fell, and General Motors began to challenge Ford for automobile industry leadership. The British car company Vauxhall was taken over in 1925 (General Motors also talked to Austin, but did not finalize a deal), and the German company Opel was absorbed in 1928. Pontiac grew out of Oakland in 1926 and replaced it completely from 1931.

By the 1930s, Chevrolet was the fastest-selling car in the United States with Oldsmobile, Pontiac and Buick all well established in the 'top ten' league table. Not only that, but Cadillac still set high standards for quality and engineering, and was one of America's very best cars. General Motors' cars were being built in factories spread all around the United States – the corporation was in a dominant position, one it would maintain over the decades to come, in spite of the Industry's fluctuating fortunes.

Motoring for Fun

The birth of the sports car

THE early progress of automobile design can easily be summarized: in the 1880s engineers struggled to make automobiles go at all, in the 1890s they made them go reliably, and in the 1900s they made them go beautifully. But it was not until the machines had proved they were reliable – and at the same time predictable – that they could be used for pleasure.

What is a sports car? There is no easy description. In the 1900s, however, it would be true to say that most pioneer drivers were also sportsmen – they had to be, to put up with the discomforts that the driving of the period entailed. Perhaps it is simplest to suggest that a car which could be used for fun was, automatically, a sports car.

In the beginning, to use a high-performance car on near-deserted roads must have been sheer heaven. Or was it? If those roads were not in poor condition, or plagued by dust, and if there were no punctures to be mended, if there was no need to search desperately for gasoline, and no need to look around for repairs, perhaps it was. . .

In Britain, too, there was the problem of the overall open-road speed limit of 12mph before 1904 and 20mph thereafter. This was ruthlessly and rigidly enforced by the police, and the local magistrates were often viciously anti-driver in their judgment.

LEFT: *Early sports cars in the German Prince Henry Trials of 1908. Even though this photograph is 80 years old, the sports car 'line' is already obvious.*

RIGHT: *A very early example of a Bugatti – the Type 10 of 1908. Bugatti was to be in the forefront of auto design for the next 30 years.*

BELOW: *Several American manufacturers took up the fashionable 'raceabout' style in the 1910s – this being the well-known Mercer marque.*

ABOVE: *This Amilcar Type CO of 1926 was one of several French sports cars which starred in the 1920s, then faded rapidly away.*

LEFT: *The MG M-Type Midget of 1929/30.*

RIGHT: *A between-wars Frazer Nash.*

Nowadays we might think of a typical sports car as a Corvette, an MG MGA or a Porsche 356 – all cars with smallish engines, compact packaging and agile road behavior. In the years before World War I, however, a sports car – in other words, a car for sporting use – was very different from that. The cars that set the trend were those massive-engined two-seaters used in the town-to-town races, in the Gordon Bennett races, and in the first British Tourist Trophy events. Mostly these were rakish models looking, sounding and going a lot faster than their 'touring' equivalents.

The very fast Mercedes car, the 1901 35hp model which dominated proceedings at the Nice Speed Week in 1901, was one such, and it inspired a rush of imitators in the next few years. The Mercedes, like its rivals from Panhard, Mors and De Dietrich, had a big and lusty four-cyclinder engine. It was only after Napier made the layout fashionable that six-cylinder cars also came along.

At that point in history, too, even companies like British Daimler and Rolls-Royce produced fast sporting machines, and with cars like the big 70hp Thomas Flyers, the Italas and the Métallurgiques also available, there was no lack of choice. But only, please note, for the wealthy.

Until about 1906 or 1907 there was really very little difference between a fast sports car and pure racing car, but once the French introduced Grand Prix racing and countries like Germany began promoting long open-road races or trials for road cars, the two types moved steadily apart. Indeed, the one event that saw the birth of the definitive two-seater sports car was the 1907 *Kaiserpreis* race, which was a four 70-mile lap event in the Taunus mountains of Germany. It was a race won by Felice Nazzaro's Fiat, but there was also much competition from Benz and Daimler.

After the last of the three Herkomer events was held in Bavaria, Prince Henry of Prussia sponsored a new series of trials to replace it. In 1908, and starting from Berlin, the first such contest saw specially designed 'Prince Henry' models developed. Within two years, Ferdinand Porsche had designed a Prince Henry Austro-Daimler, and shortly afterwards Laurence H Pomeroy also designed a Prince Henry Vauxhall for the same purpose.

Meanwhile, in the United States, American manufacturers developed the *Kaiserpreis* style of car a stage further, into what we now know as characteristic 'raceabout' models.

Of the many imitators of this fashion, some of the best known came from Locomobile (the Model H of 1905-09), Lozier (Type I), Mercer (the Raceabout) and Stutz (the Bearcat). This type of car stayed in vogue until the mid-1910s.

The definition of the sports car was now changing, to accommodate smaller, lighter and altogether more nimble two-seaters. From France in 1910 came the first of the series-production Bugattis, the Type 13 (later known as the Brescia), from Spain in 1911 the nicely detailed 3.6-liter Hispano-Suiza Alfonso model, and from Britain the 4.5-liter Talbot 25/50 model of 1914. Even the prototype Aston Martin was on the road before World War I, though sales did not begin until 1921.

In the 1920s, of course, sports cars became more and more popular, their sales increasing as fast as their size, bulk and prices fell. Not only did Bentley begin building their massive race-winning creations, but firms like Amilcar, Chenard-Walcker, Salmson and Delage of France, Alvis, Invicta, GN and Frazer Nash of Britain, Alfa Romeo and Lancia of Italy, all joined in. It was a wondrous sporting decade which established the sports car pedigree for all time.

The Car at War

The Western Front, 1914-1918

IN war, as in peace, before the automobile was developed the most important mode of transportation was the horse. Horses were either used to tow gun carriages, ambulances and carts full of supplies and ammunition, or were ridden with great style by famous cavalry regiments. From 1914, all that changed.

World War I, in any case, really started in a car. On 28 June 1914, the heir to the throne of Austria-Hungary, Archduke Franz Ferdinand, was being driven to a civic reception at the Town Hall, Sarajevo, in an open Graf und Stift. An assassin's bullet killed him, the Hapsburg dynasty was shattered, and this precipitated the outbreak of the war.

The American Civil War had suggested the awesome destructive power of the machine gun, and the Boer War had seen both the world's first armored car and an armored steam tractor (a Fowler, which pulled armored wagons), but it was not until World War I that a conflict was eventually settled by the use of machines. At sea battleships, destroyers and submarines were all-important, in the air the airplane took over from the observation balloon, and on land we saw the first highly mobile armored cars, tanks and, of course, staff cars.

It still seems incongruous today that the first successful armored car was based on the Rolls-Royce 40/50hp chassis. The Belgians started the trend by armoring some Minervas, but the British soon joined in, with armored cars (sometimes adding three tons of steel) on the Rolls-Royce and Lanchester chassis. The chassis was at once rugged enough and powerful enough to accept armored bodywork, and with machine guns mounted on top it was a formidable new weapon of war.

Such machines, of course, were only really useful where the war was a mobile one – East Africa and the Middle East being perfect examples – but wherever the opposing armies dug in with trenches, they were useless. It was to surmount such obstacles that British designers, urged on by Winston Churchill, mated caterpillar tracks to armored chassis, with

RIGHT: *During World War I, Vauxhall provided the British Army with hundreds of these sturdy staff cars.*

BELOW: *To rush reinforcements to the Marne in 1914, the French government requisitioned hundreds of cars and Renault taxis for overnight transportation. Before then, armies had relied on horses, trains and their own legs.*

OPPOSITE ABOVE: *Today you know a Mack as a truck – but in 1917 the company built armored cars too.*

OPPOSITE: *Armored cars were built for the Belgian army by Peugeot and Mors.*

ABOVE: *The tank was invented during World War I. These are French-built tanks of the US Army in the Argonne forest in 1918.*

guns, thus inventing the tank. Early tanks were cumbersome, slow and unreliable, but they were to become the most important piece in any modern nation's military jigsaw.

Even so, at the beginning of the war, it was only the 'Top Brass' who had automobiles, for the British Army owned a grand total of 80 vehicles – consisting of both cars and lorries – at the time.

Suddenly, in September 1914, the automobile played a vital role. The German Army broke through along the Marne, and in order to rush reinforcements to plug the gap, the military governor of Paris requisitioned every one of the Paris taxis. Thus it was that one variety of Renault, the Type AG two-cylinder 8hp, became the famous 'Taxi of the Marne', as a fleet of 600 carried thousands of troops to the front, where a successful mission was accomplished.

There was so much movement in modern warfare, and the fronts were so lengthy, that the generals could no longer get around on horseback. Most of the senior officers in the British Expeditionary Force were supplied with Rolls-Royce 40/50hp models, unarmored. It is known that Field Marshal

Sir John French had a Barker-bodied limousine, while General Joffre (his opposite number in the French Army) had a cabriolet version. The German equivalent to the Rolls-Royce, as used by Field Marshal von Hindenburg, was a huge 21-liter Benz Tourer. A number of big and expensive cars were donated to the war effort by their patriotic owners, some of whom came along to act as chauffeurs.

The Rolls-Royce, however, was only intended for the chosen few. Most generals had to make do with sturdy cars like the Prince Henry 25hp Vauxhalls of the period, sleeve-valve Daimlers, the well-liked 16hp and 20hp Sunbeams, plus some Wolseleys, Austins or Singers. Where the British used motorcycles for the speedy sending of messages, the French chose to use Bébé Peugeots.

Before long, however, the motor vehicle was everywhere. In 1914, in a great rush (the outbreak of war, although expected fatalistically by all the politicians, had certainly not been planned for) 6000 vehicles were somehow gathered together for use on the French front. By November 1918 that figure had risen to no fewer than 92,000 vehicles.

Although Detroit's Henry Ford was a pacifist, his British, French and Canadian factories were soon turned to building specially equipped Model Ts by the thousand, along with light trucks. Other car-makers, British, American, French and Italian, not only turned to making military versions of their cars, but also turned their hand to making aircraft engines and other such parts.

In this way, as in so many others, the automobile changed the face of the world.

Whatever Happened to. . .?

The cars which lost their way

DO you remember Duesenberg, Cord and Auburn? Do you recall De Dion, Sunbeam and Delage? Whatever happened to the *real* Bentley? To Darracq and to Marmon? It's all very sad – between the two World Wars, some of the great names of the earlier years of the automobile disappeared. But why, and how?

One distinguished American automobile historian, Beverley Rae Kimes, once noted that there were thousands of American makes of car which had not survived to the present day. However, what is surprising is that some of the most famous names also died away in the years between the wars.

Consider the first four makes of car to be put on sale – Benz, Daimler, Panhard et Lavassor and Peugeot. The last German Daimler was built in 1902, just a year after the new Mercedes marque was adopted. Benz disappeared in favour of the Mercedes-Benz. Panhard et Levassor became Panhard almost at once, was taken over by Citroën in 1964, and breathed its last in 1967. Only Peugeot, now the dominant member of the Peugeot-Citroën-Talbot combine, has survived to the present day.

Even some of the biggest names in North America – those included in the General Motors and Chrysler combines of the 1920s and 1930s – also disappeared. One early name in General Motors was that of Oakland, a company which gave birth to Pontiac, but was eventually supplanted by its offspring. General Motors also invented the La Salle in 1927, as a cheaper type of Cadillac, but this too disappeared in 1940.

The original Chrysler group included the Maxwell, which dated from 1904, but it vanished in 1925. Not at all dismayed, Chrysler then invented De Soto in 1928, as a rather cheaper model, and this soldiered on until 1960.

Every marque which died had a different reason for doing so. In the case of Bentley, the firm set up by WO Bentley after

GK 6661

RIGHT: *Duesenberg was launched in 1920 but died in 1937, killed by the Depression. This 1925 Model A was an early 'classic.'*

OPPOSITE BELOW: *The supercharged 4½-liter Bentley was the most famous of these 'vintage' models. Rolls-Royce bought the name in 1931.*

BELOW: *In the 1920s Lanchester built excellent cars. These are 40hp models of 1924 and 1925.*

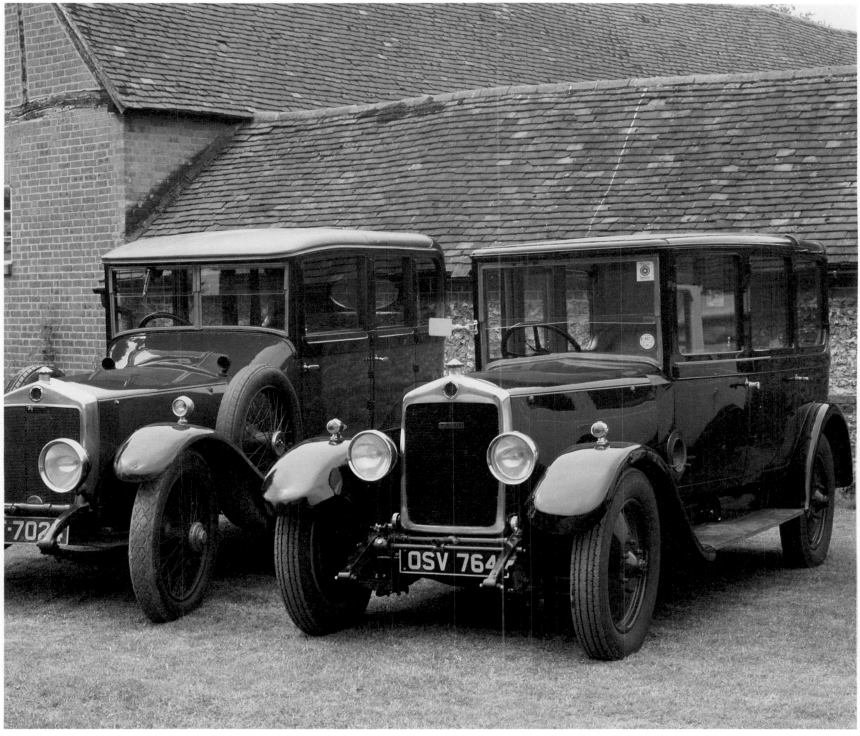

OPPOSITE ABOVE: *Franklin built air-cooled cars from 1901 to 1934, but the public finally rejected them. This touring model dates from 1927.*

OPPOSITE: *There is no trace of air-cooling in this 1928 Type 12B Franklin Victoria*

Brougham. In the end, there was no advantage over water-cooled cars.

ABOVE: *Only two different Cord types were produced. This was the original 1929 L29 model, with straight-eight Lycoming engine and front-wheel-drive.*

World War I, the cars were always of the highest quality, reliability and performance, but buyers for these expensive machines were hard to find. The company overindulged in the expense of racing and finally ran out of money in 1931 when the Depression was at its worst. Rolls-Royce took over the name, but the company was never the same again.

Sunbeam was another British marque whose finest years were in the 1910s and 1920s. The first cars had been sold in 1901, and the great years began in 1909 when Louis Coatalen joined as chief designer. Sunbeams raced with success before World War I, provided reliable staff car transport on the Western Front, and became splendid sporting cars in the 1920s. In the 1930s the marque was dragged down by the Sunbeam-Talbot-Darracq (STD) combine's financial problems, and was taken over in receivership by Rootes in 1935.

The same fate befell Talbot, which had begun production in West London in 1903. Georges Roesch produced the six-cylinder 14/45hp in the mid-1920s and developed the design into the successful 75, 90 and 105 models in the early 1930s. By 1935 the Talbot was one of Britain's very finest cars, but the company was then laid low in the same way as Sunbeam, and Rootes bought up the corpse. One of the original French pioneers, De Dion, had a distinguished history before World War I; at one time or another, 140 other makes of car were using De Dion engines and other companies were copying

from the same design. After the war, however, fortunes declined and demand dropped, with the last cars being built in 1932. Darracq, another French pioneer, prospered until 1920, after which it joined forces with Sunbeam and Talbot, the name soon disappearing into the maw of the STD group.

Delage was a great manufacturer of the inter-war years, which not only prepared a whole range of fine, fast, *grand routier* models, but produced some outstanding Grand Prix racing cars. But the founder, Louis Delage, ran out of money in the mid-1930s as sales declined and was forced to sell out to Delahaye.

Amilcar was another French company that deserved better luck. Founded in 1921, Amilcar built a series of light and efficient sporting *voiturettes* with four-cylinder, six-cylinder and eight-cylinder engines. The Depression hit France just as hard as elsewhere, Amilcar's sales dropped away, and the last was built in 1939.

Several other famous American names did not make it into modern times, usually because their models became too expensive to sell in the Depression-hit United States. Consider Duesenberg of Indianapolis, whose name had already been made by racing before the first car was sold in 1920. The cars were always large, complex and expensive, not least the famous Model J and Model SJ eight-cylinder cars of 1928 and 1932, which were phenomenally powerful (the SJ had 320 hp). Although Duesenberg staggered on through the Depression, the company's partner Cord finally pulled them into bankruptcy.

Auburn came into existence in 1900 and built many fine cars before being taken over by EL Cord in 1924. Under his leadership larger and faster Auburns were produced, the Duesenberg company was bought up in 1928, and eight-cylinder and V12 models were announced in the early 1930s. The most amazing Auburn of all was the supercharged eight-cylinder Speedster Type 851 of 1935, with a guaranteed top speed of 100mph. But it all went very wrong in 1937 and the marque folded, another victim of the Depression.

The Cord was an offshoot of the Auburn and Duesenberg combine, with a supercharged front-wheel drive, eight-cylinder car, the L-29, in 1929 and a Duesenberg-inspired car, the front-wheel-drive Model 810, in 1935. The problem was that these cars were both expensive and unfamiliar to American buyers. Cord died along with Auburn and Duesenberg in 1937.

Companies come and companies go. . .

BELOW: *Delage of France built some fine Grand Touring cars in the 1920s and 1930s. This 1934 D8-15S had an eight-cylinder engine, and near-100mph top speed.*

RIGHT: *The Invicta was a typical British 'vintage' car, made only between 1925 and 1935. This 4½-liter S was a successful sports car.*

Ford's Model T

A car 'for the man in the street'

ALTHOUGH Henry Ford built his very first car, the Quadricycle, in 1896, it was not until 1908 that his still-small company launched the Model T. This not only transformed the Ford company, but completely changed the face of transportation in the United States. Between 1908 and 1927 more than 15 million Model Ts were produced. setting a record that stood for more than 40 years.

Ford's original cars, like the four-cylinder Model B of 1904 and the six-cylinder Model K that followed it, were expensive, but Henry Ford always had a dream of selling masses of cars at low prices to the 'man in the street.' It needed a disagreement with his co-directors, and the buying out of several of them, before Henry got his way. The Model T, priced at $850, was eventually launched on 1 October 1908.

BELOW: *Almost single-handed, the Model T Ford turned motoring from a rich man's hobby to everyday transport. At its height more than two million Model T Fords were built in the space of a single year.*

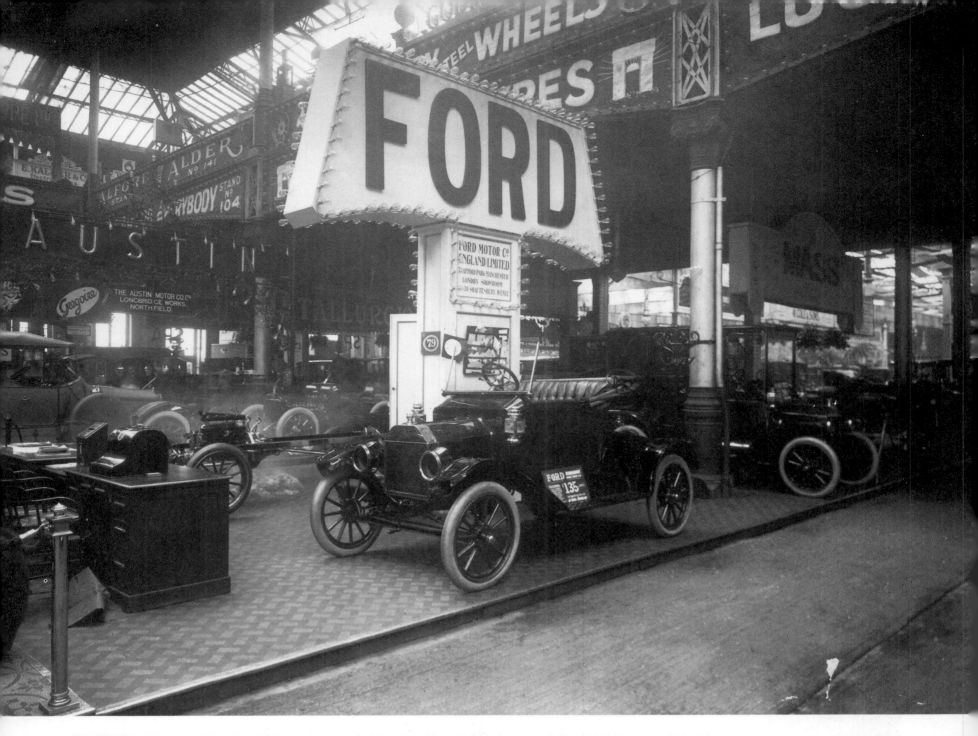

ABOVE: *Once the Model T was established in the USA, Henry Ford set up other assembly factories all over the world. One of the largest was at Trafford Park, in England. This shows the British company's Motor Show display, at Olympia in 1912, when the price was a mere £135.*

LEFT: *Model Ts eventually came in all shapes and sizes. This station wagon type was built in 1921, when the T was climbing to the peak of its popularity.*

RIGHT: *Yet another variation on a well-used theme – this was a Model T delivery van, built in 1916, and lovingly restored in the 1980s.*

In the next few years, Model T motoring grew to be so popular that the car became a part of the American dream, as *familiar as Coca Cola, as ubiquitous as the air which* Americans breathed, and seemingly adaptable to almost every purpose. Henry liked to call the Model T a 'universal car,' for in the beginning he thought it could go on selling for ever. Apart from body styles being gradually, but almost imperceptibly, updated, the chassis changed very little indeed; one could certainly buy spare parts for a mid-1920s Model T and fit them straight on to a 1909 model.

In its original styling, the Model T looked similar to several other spidery touring cars of the period. However, that distinctive brass radiator style soon made it stand out, as did its easily recognizable put-putting exhaust note. The chassis layout was simple in the extreme, not only because Ford wanted to make the Model T as easily repairable in Nebraska as New York, or in Delaware as in Detroit.

Front and rear suspension was by transverse leaf springs, with the axles located by radius arms, and because of the *exceptional ground clearance a Model T could pick its way* over – and through – the most appalling terrain. The engine itself was a simple but rugged side-valve four-cylinder design, backed by an idiosyncratic epicyclic transmission.

All in all, the Model T was an intriguing mixture of the archaic and the advanced. The transmission, for instance, might be unique and require the 'clutch' pedal to be used as a means of shifting gear, but there was no gearshift as such, and there were only two forward ratios. As with other cars, there were three foot pedals, but the right pedal operated the transmission drum brake, the center pedal engaged reverse and the left pedal operated the shift itself. The accelerator control was a stalk on the steering column, one of the strange features of Henry Fords Model T.

RIGHT: Although the Model T's engine was a simple four-cylinder side-valve unit, it was matched to a complex epicyclic transmission. Of the three pedals, the left one operated the gear shift, the center engaged reverse, and the right the transmission brake.

Mercedes-Benz

Setting a standard for others to follow

IN spite of fierce competition, the humiliating aftermath of World War I, and the economic blizzard that engulfed Germany in the early 1920s, two proud car-making companies – Daimler and Benz – held on to their stability and actually increased their standing in the world of the automobile. However, few companies had enough resources, or enough guaranteed sales, to make it through hyper-inflation without help, and in the end the two German giants had to get together to survive. In 1924 Daimler and Benz agreed to cooperate in some respects, and in 1926 a formal merger was arranged.

Thereafter, the company became known as Daimler-Benz and the products were always marketed as Mercedes-Benz.

The plain three-pointed (Daimler) star atop the radiators was replaced by a three-pointed star surrounded by a laurel wreath and labelled 'Mercedes-Benz.'

For some years, cars continued to be made in two locations, at the Daimler factories in Stuttgart and at the old Benz plant in Mannheim. It was not until the 1930s that all car assembly was concentrated on Stuttgart, and it was not until after World War II that chassis and final assembly lines were moved to the previous body-construction factory at Sindelfingen on the outskirts of the city.

Daimler-Benz's most obvious assets were its design engineers, for the new board of management included three truly famous personalities – Dr Ferdinand Porsche and Fritz Nallinger from Daimler, and Hans Nibel from Benz. It was no wonder that there were both outstanding new products and enormous boardroom battles to come, in the next few years.

The most exciting late-1920s Mercedes-Benz cars were the supercharged six-cylinder models that Porsche had started to evolve when he joined Daimler a few years earlier. These all featured supercharging that could be 'clutched' into operation by an emphatic movement of the throttle foot, a process which was usually accompanied by the scream of the hard-working engine.

This design started life with a 100hp engine (140hp with supercharger engaged), which explains its original title of 24/100/140, but within a few years the engine had been

BELOW: *In 1901 Daimler introduced the new, low-slung Mercedes range. This is a 120hp derivative of 1905.*

OPPOSITE: *Mercedes used motor sport to develop, and to publicize its models, here a 1922 Targa Florio.*

OPPOSITE BELOW: *Edwardian Mercedes cars, like this example, had flat radiators, and three-pointed star badges.*

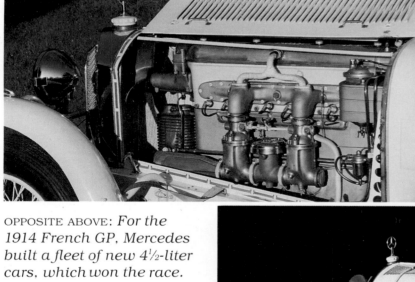

OPPOSITE ABOVE: *For the 1914 French GP, Mercedes built a fleet of new 4½-liter cars, which won the race.*

OPPOSITE: *The most famous pre-1914 Benz is the massive 200hp 'Blitzen' model, which had a 21.5-liter engine.*

TOP: *The most famous of Dr Porsche's supercharged 'sixes' built for Mercedes – the SSK model.*

ABOVE: *Seven liters of supercharged 38/250 'SS' engine.*

RIGHT: *The Mercedes-Benz SS, or 38/250 model, had a blown 7-liter six-cylinder engine.*

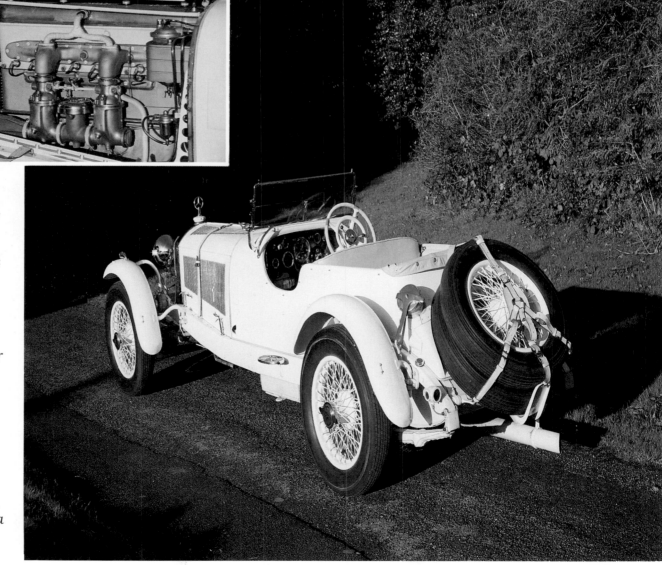

enlarged to no less than 7 liters and boosted still further. The chassis design was shortened, lowered and made lighter, with the result that the exclusive SSK sports car had ratings of 170/225hp and a top speed of more than 100mph, while the ultra-light SSKL (L for *Leicht*) could dispose of up to 300hp in race-car trim.

Porsche, meanwhile, had left Daimler-Benz after a blazing row with his fellow directors, so it was Hans Nibel who was responsible for the next Mercedes-Benz 'Supercar.' If the previous cars had already set standards for others to follow, this one took the marque even farther ahead.

The flagship, launched in 1930, was the Type 770 Grosser-model, a monster intended for use by politicians, potentates and tycoons. It was an enormous car, with typically flamboyant coachwork, and was powered by a straight eight-cylinder engine of 7.7 liters with the well-proven type of 'optional' supercharging. Customers included ex-Kaiser Wilhelm II of Germany and Emperor Hirohito of Japan.

Its successor, produced only in 1938 and 1939 for Nazi party bosses and their lackeys to use, was another 770 Grosser, still with the same engine (and up to 230hp when supercharged), but with a new tubular chassis frame, independent front suspension and De Dion rear suspension (all inspired by Grand Prix Mercedes-Benz models of the day). Not only did it look impressive, but it weighed up to 8000 pounds (with *no* power steering), could reach 110 mph, and rarely recorded more than 5 miles per gallon. Only 88 such cars were built.

Daimler-Benz also produced a series of flamboyant supercharged six-cylinder cars (the 500K and 540K Series) during

the 1930s, which were really softened-down, rather 'trans-atlantic' successors to the SSK models. But the company's most significant contribution to automobile engineering in the 1930s was in the realm of quantity-production cars.

In 1931 the new Type 170 was revealed, not only with a box section chassis at a time when most rivals were still using channel frames, but with independent front *and* rear suspension. A few years later the development of this advanced chassis was mated to the world's first passenger-car diesel engine, a 2.6-liter unit which naturally led to it being called the Type 260D.

Not only that, but in the mid-1930s Hans Nibel's design team finally came round to Porsche's thinking and produced a rear-engined car for sale. This was the Type 130H (H for *Heck*, or 'Rear'), which had a 1.3-liter engine and only 26hp,

but still had rather unmanageable handling characteristics; later the larger-engined 170H was also produced. The limited-production 150H was in fact a mid-engined 55hp overhead-cam 1.5-liter sports derivative of this layout, but very few were made. By comparison, the front-engined 170V of the late 1930s was an enormous success, with more than 90,000 vehicles being built before car production was stopped in 1942.

All this helped boost Mercedes-Benz output to unheard-of heights. About 28,000 cars a year were being assembled by 1938. At the same time the company was also dominating the truck markets, and with its excellent V12 aero-engines was preparing to supply power to the Luftwaffe's fighters and bombers. By any reckoning the between-wars Daimler-Benz concern was a standard-setter for the rest of Europe.

LEFT: *In 1930, Mercedes-Benz launched the Type 770 Grosser-model, with supercharged 7.6-liter engine, producing up to 200hp. There was a six-speed gearbox, and some cars weighed nearly 6000lb. Only 117 cars of this type were built; this particular chauffeur-driven example was supplied to ex-Kaiser Wilhelm II.*

98082

Races of the Titans

The heroic days of motor racing

THE world's first car race took place in June 1895, from Paris to Bordeaux and back. Over 732 miles the average speed of the winning 1.2-liter Panhard was a mere 15 mph. From that point on, racing car performance, engine sizes and power all increased dramatically. Five years later the Paris-Toulouse road race of 837 miles was won at 40.2mph by a massive Mors. There was much more to come in the next few years.

Between 1900 and 1914 racing car performance leaped ahead yet again, so much so that the sport's rule-makers periodically attempted to slow the cars down. The problem was that straight-line performance far exceeded roadholding standards and the braking of the machines. Racing cars, in short, were dangerous projectiles that could only be controlled by a few brave men.

LEFT: *The very first Grand Prix was held near Le Mans in June 1906. The two-day race was 770 miles long and cars had to weigh less than 2204lb.*

ABOVE: *The British Tourist Trophy races were for road-equipped sporting cars. Here an 18hp Gladiator holds off a 20hp Vulcan in the 1908 event.*

In the early 1900s there were no permanent racing circuits and the vogue was for town-to-town races. These were straightforward dashes from point to point, on public roads, where animals, railway crossings and, above all, the populace were great hazards. In general, the roads were loose-surfaced and every competing car set up rooster-tails of dust behind it through which following drivers had to steer almost by instinct.

Designers and entrants closed their eyes to potential carnage and built monstrous cars to do the job. Panhard's 1902

race car was a 13.7-liter machine, while the Mors which *averaged* 65.3mph in the 1903 Paris-Madrid race had a 70hp 11.2-liter engine. For the time being, however, the accidents and the deaths caused on the first section of the Paris-Madrid event brought an end to town-to-town racing (the race itself was, in fact, stopped at Bordeaux, the cars returning to Paris by train).

It was time to bring racing under better supervision and the French, who were already in control of the sport worldwide, invented Grand Prix racing in 1906. For a number of years the French Grand Prix was the only race that mattered, and around it manufacturers were obliged to build cars to a particular formula. It was expensive, but so much prestige was at stake that there was no shortage of entries.

In the next eight years the authorities imposed six different formulae, ranging from one requiring a maximum weight to one requiring a minimum weight, maximum fuel

consumption, maximum engine size, maximum vehicle width, and even a maximum engine piston requirement. None of this really worked, for cars became faster and faster, and to get round the rules designers made engines more and more efficient.

The very first Grand Prix was held over a 65-mile triangular road circuit near Le Mans in June 1906. All 32 cars weighed less than 1000kg (2204 pounds), and all had engines of between 12 and 18 liters. One of the quirks of the rules was that only the driver and his riding mechanic could work on the car when it needed repair or tire-changing. Ferenc Szisz's Renault won the event, taking more than 12 hours to complete the 770 miles at an average of 63mph; his winning margin over Nazzaro's Fiat was no less than 32 minutes.

With virtually the same cars but a different road circuit (this time near Dieppe), race speeds rose to 70.5mph in 1907, so for 1908 a 'maximum piston area' regulation was imposed. If it was meant to reduce speeds, it failed. The 1908 Grand Prix, once again held at Dieppe, saw Mercedes produce a four-cylinder 12.8-liter machine with 120hp; driven by Christian Lautenschlager, it averaged 69mph.

Such cars looked and sounded magnificent. The Mercedes had a four-cylinder engine with separate header pipes poking out through the side of the hood, chain drive, and two slim spare wheels clamped to the tail behind the two-seater cockpit. The top speed was at least 100mph — and there were no front-wheel brakes.

Grand Prix racing then fell into limbo for three years, notably because the French could not stomach 'their' race being won by foreign cars (an Italian Fiat in 1907, a German Mercedes in 1908). In those years, however, other forms of racing allowed engines to become even more powerful, so there was no hope of containing the performance of pure-bred machines for long. When the French Grand Prix was revived for 1912, the authorities washed their hands of this aim, and for no obvious reason merely specified a maximum width for the cars, which limited the wheel tracks and, presumably, the roadholding.

In that year, Peugeot startled everyone with the first-ever application of dual overhead camshafts and four valves per cylinder, all in a 7.6-liter engine producing 130hp, while Fiat

ABOVE: *Interested spectators watch the winning De Dietrich during the ill-fated Paris-Madrid race of 1903.*

OPPOSITE ABOVE: *In mainland Britain, all the early long-distance races were held at the Brooklands track. This is the Davis/Dunfee 'works'*

Bentley Speed Six in the 1930 'Double Twelve' event.

OPPOSITE: *The first Monaco GP (1929) was won by Grover-Williams's Type 35 Bugatti.*

and Lorraine-Dietrich produced cars with 15-liter engines, Fiat claiming no less than 200hp for their monster.

This 'race of the Titans' was held over the familiar Dieppe circuit, with two days' racing of 477 miles each. Eventually new technology defeated sheer horsepower, with the 'small' Peugeot of Georges Boillot winning at 68.45mph, though Louis Wagner's Fiat was never far behind.

The 1913 race was held over a 19.5 mile course near Amiens, the 29 laps having to be completed in a day. This time a maximum fuel-consumption formula (14.2 miles per gallon) was imposed, so Peugeot produced a 5.65-liter version of the 1912 car that easily met the fuel consumption rules, and Boillot again won easily at 72.2mph.

The last pre-war Grand Prix was over a hilly 23.3 mile circuit near Lyons. It was run to a 4.5-liter engine formula and was totally dominated by Mercedes. That company, which was never known to attack any project in a half-hearted manner, used aero-engine technology and a single-cam engine layout to produce 115hp and to give a maximum speed of 112mph.

The Mercedes drivers practiced for weeks ahead of the race. Five examples started the race and three of them finished first, second and third. It is said that the French spectators were so shattered and humiliated by all this that: 'no cheer was raised, and no hands clapped as the three Mercedes crossed the finishing line.'

Four weeks later, France was at war with Germany. The racing 'Age of the Titans' was over.

ABOVE: *Four generations of successful British land speed records. From the bottom: 350hp Sunbeam; twin-engined '1000hp' Sunbeam of 1927; Golden Arrow of 1929; the 1964 gas-turbined Bluebird.*

BELOW: *Malcolm (later Sir Malcolm) Campbell sits inside the 350hp Sunbeam Land Speed Record car of 1924.*

The Vintage Car

A European phenomenon

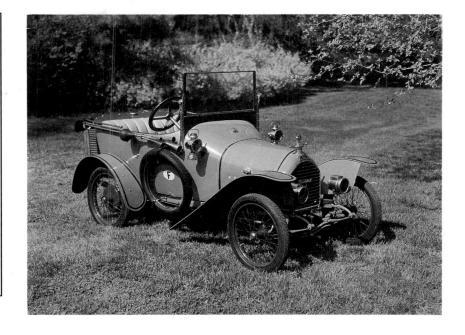

THE phrase 'vintage car' was not invented until 1934, when a new British automobile club was founded. The enthusiasts who joined to set up this organization were all bound together by the same beliefs – that the best cars in the world had been produced between the close of World War I and the end of 1930, and that no worthwhile cars had been produced since then.

ABOVE: *A typical European car of the early 1920s, the French-manufactured Peugeot 'Bébé.'*

BELOW: *Citroën's first cars were sold in 1919, and for years were simple, solid, no-nonsense vintage machines. This was a 5CV of 1923.*

Having decided to worship only one age of the automobile (and who is to say whether such enthusiasts were misguided?), the cars had to be defined and the club given a name. Since it was thought that these cars were the best, the vocabulary of fine wines was 'borrowed.' The cars became 'vintage' and the club the Vintage Sports Car Club (VSCC).

To anyone living outside Europe, and especially to any enthusiast in North America, the phrase 'vintage car' has very little meaning. Americans have their own ideas of what constitutes a fine car, and to them such a car is a 'classic' if it was built between 1925 and 1948, dates that in turn mean very little to Europeans.

Officially, therefore, a vintage car is one built between 1919 and the end of 1930, though this rigid definition brings all kinds of anomalies in its wake. Presumably we must assume that a Rolls-Royce Phantom II built in 1929 or 1930 is vintage, but that one built in 1934 or 1935 is not? Strange — especially as the later models in any series tend to be better built than the originals.

It is worth mentioning, however, another VSCC category, the 'post-vintage thoroughbred', which allows fine cars of the 1930s to have some semblance of respectability. Sports cars like the Meadows-engined Lagondas, some Frazer Nashes and some Aston Martins qualify.

Everyone has their own idea of what a typical vintage car looks like, goes like and, above all, feels like. Vintage motoring is not merely measured by 0-60mph figures, by sizes, weights and shapes, but by character. The vintage movement favors those cars that were built by craftsmen, often in relatively small workshops, and in limited numbers. But the definition of 'vintage' is so all-embracing that it covers a hand-built Bentley and a mass-produced Austin Seven, a Type 35 Bugatti racing car and a workaday Morris 'bullnose' model. The sheer variety of fine cars built in this period is astonishing — and all count as vintage.

Let us look at the anatomy of a typical vintage car — the 'bullnose' Morris of the early and mid-1920s. This typifies what a vintage car, and vintage motoring, is all about.

The basis of a 'bullnose' was a rather whippy, separate chassis, mounted above the line of the axles throughout, with a forged-section front axle and a welded 'banjo' rear axle. Front and rear suspension was by half-elliptic leaf springs, and damping was by adjustable Hartford friction shock absorbers.

A 'bullnose' was steered by worm and wheel, with a long straight steering column leading back into the driving compartment. Wheels were detachable steel 'artillery-style', fitted with narrow 'balloon' tires. By the mid-1920s there were front and rear drum brakes, operated by a foot pedal or a hand lever, all being intricately connected, balanced and counterbalanced by rods, levers and cross-shafts.

The side-valve four-cylinder engine was mounted well back in the frame, there was a simple single-plate clutch, and a four-speed transmission, with a long gearshift growing straight up out of the top cover.

The 'bullnose,' like most vintage cars, was sold with a choice of body styles. All used the same front end and characteristic radiator, but there were many variations aft of the windshield. All were simply built of metal or fabric panels affixed to a wooden body-skeleton, with minimal protection against corrosion. They had front and rear fenders connected by stout running boards. The headlamps were free-standing, between the radiator and the fenders. The spare wheel was usually clamped to the tail, but sometimes tucked into a well on one of the running boards.

Windshields, without exception, were lofty and vertical, often with opening sections to allow better visibility on rainy days. Whether the cars were two-seater or four-seater tourers, four/five-seater sedans, or some variation on the theme, there was usually a generous amount of leg room, but rather

TOP: *Not only a well-known vintage car, but a vintage sports car — the Alvis 12/50 was a smart and lively 1½-liter four-cylinder British car.*

ABOVE: *Vincenzo Lancia founded his Italian firm in 1906, and built many fine vintage sports cars. This is a 1929 'Torpedo' bodied Lambda.*

OPPOSITE ABOVE: *Love them or hate them — it doesn't matter — the Ford Motor Company's Model T was the typical American vintage car of the 1920s.*

OPPOSITE: *Some of the finest vintage sports cars were of French manufacture. This was a 1930 example of the Delage D8, with bodywork by Chapron.*

restricted width. The rear seats were usually on top of the line of the back axle, making a high roof line essential. (As car styles changed in the next 20 years or so, the width inside a body gradually increased, while the amount of sprawling room, especially in the rear seats, was gradually reduced.)

A sports car with a small engine – such as an Aston Martin or a Bugatti – was altogether lower, narrower, and very rarely sold with any other than a two-seater style, while large-engined sports cars like the archetypal vintage Bentleys were as lofty as any sedan, very bulky and very heavy.

All, however, had the same sort of 'feel' about them. The shift mechanism was positive, if not light, the steering was direct, if not necessarily easy, the engines solidly reliable. Bodies were practical, solid and quite devoid of 'flash.' Equipment was complete where fittings were essential and there was nothing to make the ensemble vulgar. There was, indeed, a rightness about a good vintage car – a rightness that was soon to be lost.

What happened in the 1930s? With the advent of a new ability to press compound curves into large pieces of sheet-metal came the one-piece steel turret-top, full-width styling and, eventually, unitary construction. In brief, cost-saving took precedence over quality, gimmicks over practicality and mass-production over craftsmanship. Perhaps the founder members of the VSCC had something, after all?

Motoring Tycoons and their Cars

Royce, Sloan, Morris and Ford

TOP: *Henry Royce (with beard) was Rolls-Royce's technical chief for nearly 30 years. Ernest Hives, to his left, later became the company's chairman.*

ABOVE: *Alfred P Sloan brought order to General Motors in the 1920s, and inspired the birth of this successful type of Chevrolet.*

LOOK around the automobile industry today and it's run by corporate boards; the buccaneering pioneers like Durant and Cord are gone; the engineers-turned-entrepreneur like Henry Ford and Walter Chrysler have passed as well.

Yet the birth of almost every one of the world's outstanding marques was inspired by one man, who went on to dominate his firm for a good many years. Consider famous car names like Rolls-Royce, Ford, Opel, Honda and Chrysler — these all stemmed from the personalities behind them. It is a sad fact, though, that when the founder died or retired, there was rarely another member of his family ready to take over.

The largest companies of all — General Motors, Nissan, Volkswagen and Fiat — were not named after a founder, but in their formative years they all had one strong man at the top. But you are excused if you do not recall these men — that was the way it was always intended. Until the 1920s, however, there seemed to be automobile tycoons all around, and some became as famous as the cars they were building.

There is no doubt who was the most famous of all — that was Henry Ford. In spite of his apparent 'hillbilly' manners and simplistic attitudes, he never shunned the limelight. Not only was he the chief designer — the only designer, really — of the legendary Model T, but for many years he and his close family were the only shareholders in the company.

As his many biographers have discovered, Henry Ford's personality was a puzzling paradox. On the one hand there was the businessman wise enough to invest in the automobile industry's first moving assembly line and to use the successful 'bring down prices and we'll sell more cars' gambit, but on the other hand there was the naive pacifist who financed the notorious 'peace ship' initiative to Europe during World War I, in the hope that he could stop the fighting merely with a gesture.

It was Ford, too, who once referred to history as being 'mostly bunk,' yet set up the Greenfield Village and the Henry Ford Museum, in Detroit, to preserve it. And it was Ford who refused to have union recognition in his plants. He was brilliant enough to see that the Model T was exactly what the American public needed, but blind enough not to see that it was obsolete by 1927. His thinking never moved with the times, and if it had not been for the rush of contracts gained to build military machinery during World War II, the company might not have survived the 1940s.

His son, Edsel, died young, and it was his grandson, Henry Ford II, who put the company back on an even keel once again in the post-war years.

Ford's real rival in Detroit in the 1920s was Alfred P. Sloan, the guiding genius behind the steady rise of General Motors. The company had been founded in 1908, but was a muddled mess of several competing businesses when Sloan became executive vice-president in 1921. In the next decade he shook out the whole group, systematized it, saw it buy overseas subsidiaries and take over market leadership from Ford. Before long GM was the world's largest industrial company. In every way, it was Sloan's lasting epitaph, for after he had gone from the chief executive's chair in 1946, General Motors came to be ruled by a succession of faceless men — few of whom will be remembered outside of the industry.

ABOVE: *Henry Ford controlled every aspect of his own company until the mid-1940s, although not always with wisdom or foresight.*

BELOW: *To replace the obsolete Model T, Ford rushed through the all-new, conventional Model A in 1927. This is a 1929 version.*

America's Great Depression

Boom to bust, then boom again

COMPARED with France and Germany, the United States automobile industry was late on the scene, but it made up for this with huge expansion in the 1910s and 1920s. Then came the Wall Street Crash of October 1929, which changed everything.

Once the American stock market collapsed, so did the American economy and business confidence in general. In 1927 the North American automobile industry had produced three million cars, and in 1928 this roared ahead to four million. The peak figure, in 1929, was four and a half million; four out of five cars built anywhere in the world were being produced in North America. Then came the Crash, sales plummeted, stocks of unsold cars rose rapidly and many garage businesses plunged into bankruptcy. The 1929 record would not be beaten for another 20 years.

For automobile enthusiasts who were unaffected by such financial traumas, there was the sight of gloriously engineered new cars arriving on the American scene just as

BELOW: *The magnificent eight-cylinder Duesenberg Model J arrived at exactly the wrong moment in America's industrial history . . .*

INSET: *Everything about the L-29 Cord was superlative – eight-cylinder engine, front-wheel-drive and a $3000 price – but it was badly timed for the Wall Street Crash of 1929.*

feet economically and to regain its self-confidence once   Springfield, Massachusetts, factory in 1931.

The big names fought their way through, though the pecking order changed somewhat. Ford, having lost the sales lead to Chevrolet during the Depression, was well on top during the late 1930s (mainly because of the new V8 engine and remarkably low prices).

The Ford group, however, lost ground to the Chrysler Corporation, which had been newly founded in the 1920s, and which overtook it. Ford's problem was that it was still ruled by the quixotic founder and lacked a proper range of cars. Chrysler also had Plymouth, Dodge and De Soto to sell — which they did, in profusion.

As the traditional names faded away, America's 'top people' were reduced to a choice of just three fine cars —

Lincoln, Packard and Cadillac. And once the lovely old Model K Lincoln died and Packard moved down market, the Cadillac was left on its own.

One way to sum up Detroit's problems in the 1930s is by noting that there were 31 separate marques in 1930, but only 17 by 1942 (when private car production closed down on the outbreak of war). Another way, though, is to recall that the nation pulled steadily out of the Depression and was building 3.7 million cars a year again by 1936. Boom to bust to boom again in only seven years? Only the American automobile business could have achieved such a feat of industrial reorganisation in such a short time, and with so much obvious success.

RIGHT: *Edsel Ford saw a market niche for an up-market version of the Lincoln. This was the original 4.8-liter Continental (later known as 'Mk 1') built until 1948.*

BELOW: *During the 1930s, Ford phased out the exclusive Lincolns, in favor of the Ford-derived Lincoln Zephyrs, which had side-valve V12 engines. This Model 902 was built in 1936.*

Great British Sports Cars

For the young-at-heart, everywhere

ABOVE: *To many people, the typical British sports car of the 1930s was the MG Midget. This is actually the first of the 'Nuffield' Midgets of 1936.*

The M-Type, J2, PA and PB two-seaters were eventually replaced by the MG T-Series models, which ran from 1936 to 1955. It was the TC, of 1945-50, which introduced British sports cars to the United States market, while the TD that followed was the first Midget to have independent front suspension. Even though the cars' styling changed a little over the years, all of them carried the same traditional looks with woodframed bodies, flowing fenders and easily recognizable radiators. Heaters, wind-up windows and wind-cheating styles were not provided.

To rival MG, Singer produced the Le Mans models, and Triumph produced some nice Southern Cross models, but few could match the prices. Marques such as Frazer Nash, Aston Martin and Lagonda were much more expensive.

The real boom in Great British Sports Cars came after World War II. Economic conditions made it necessary for most cars to be exported and the United States market was huge and potentially profitable, so several companies designed sports cars to appeal to that vast continent. They were, of course, sold in competition with US-built sports cars such as Mercer and Stutz.

MG, having led the way for so long, was still making the 1930s-style TD in 1952 when two new cars threatened to sweep the company away. One was the Austin-Healey 100, the other the Triumph TR2. It was not until MG's beautiful new MGA arrived in 1955 that the Abingdon-based company was back on terms. In the next two decades these cars, and their descendants, fought for every sale.

Triumph's TR2 became TR3, then TR3A, all with the same style, before the Michelotti-styled TR4 took over in 1961. This was succeeded by the TR4A in 1965, which in turn gave way

ALTHOUGH Britain certainly did not invent the sports car, it was the first country to build such machines at low prices and in large numbers. Not only MG in the 1930s, but Austin-Healey, Jaguar, MG and Triumph in the 1950s and 1960s did much to bring wind-in-the-hair driving to enthusiasts all over the world.

Cecil Kimber, and Morris Garages in Oxford, started it all in the 1920s, with their special-bodied Morris models which they christened MG. But it was the Midgets and Magnettes that followed which really popularized sports cars in Britain.

Like many of the cars that followed, these MGs were small, nimble, with rakish styling and an enormous amount of exuberant character. To keep down the costs, much of the running gear was modified from mass-production units.

87

By 1952 the original type of post-war 'split-window' Beetle was selling well, and exports to the USA were growing fast.

INSET: *The Beetle's great strength was that it could handle most road conditions with great reliability; it was exported throughout the world. This is a British model.*

ABOVE: *One of many Beetle derivatives was the smart Karmann-Ghia coupe, which was introduced in 1955.*

BELOW: *The Beetle chassis and the air-cooled engine were so rugged that the 'Dune Buggy' was invented in the USA to test the Beetle to the utmost.*

In the first few years, deliveries were confined to Europe, but by the late 1950s export traffic was going all over the world. By this time half of all VW's Beetle production went to the United States, where the car built up a faithful cult following. As with the Model T Ford of the 1920s, in the 1960s the car you were most likely to find in a New York street, a jungle village of South America or the snows of Scandinavia was a VW Beetle.

The Beetle also went into production in other countries, notably in Mexico and Brazil. It is still made in Mexico to this day. Over the years the specification improved steadily, though the styling changed little. The air-cooled 1.1-liter engine became a 1.2, a 1.3, a 1.5 and finally a 1.6-liter, the transmission got synchromesh and eventually a semi-automatic option, the front suspension was changed, the rear suspension was changed, the trunk was enlarged, and Convertible and Karmann-Ghia coupe versions were put on sale – but the basic Beetle concept stayed the same.

A squared-up style, called the Type 3 1500, was announced in 1961, but did not appeal as much as the original, though the Type 2 Transporter van derivative soon became a best-seller. Beetle sales finally passed the Model T's record in February 1972, and it was only after the new front-engined/front-drive Golf was launched in 1974 that sales dropped away.

One day, no doubt, the Beetle will die off, by which time its production total will be out of reach of every other car in the world. The Beetle is unique, in every way.

Deutschland Uber Alles

GP fireworks in the 1930s

A S we have seen, the first Grand Prix was held in 1906 and immediately attracted the attention of manufacturers anxious to promote their wares. In the early years Renault, Benz, Mercedes, Delage, Bugatti and Alfa Romeo all came to the fore. The rules changed regularly – at one time there would be a limit on engine size, at another a minimum weight would be imposed – and fortunes waxed and waned over the seasons. Each of the competing teams, however, spent its own money, for government assistance was simply not available.

Then came the 1930s, the rise of the Nazi party in Germany, and the big push to make that country supreme in everything it tackled. This, and the arrival of a new Grand Prix formula in 1934, led to some of the most stirring racing that the world has ever seen. Hitler's empire builders gave state subsidies to two companies, Auto-Union and Mercedes-Benz, to build the best racing cars in the world.

Grand Prix racing, in fact, had been in the doldrums from 1928, when a lack of interest (and spending) from Alfa Romeo and Bugatti led to 'formula libre' events being run in the early 1930s. The authorities were desperate to revitalize the sport in 1932, but it is now obvious that they then made a big mistake, for they tried to limit car performance by imposing a maximum dry weight of 750kg (1653 pounds), this to be measured without driver, fuel, oil or tires. On current experience, they reasoned that this would limit engine sizes to about 2.5 or 3.0 liters and keep performance within bounds.

They reckoned without the ingenuity, and the state-backing, of the Germans. Neither Auto-Union nor Mercedes-Benz had been involved in Grand Prix racing for many years, so they had no traditions and no existing models to confuse their thinking. Both teams built technically advanced cars with large light-alloy engines, and by 1937, when the racing was at its height, they had 6-liter engines and nearly 600hp. The sight, the sound, the smell and the performance of these cars was spectacular in every way.

Taking advantage of generous state aid, Auto-Union and Mercedes-Benz dominated GP racing from 1934 to 1939. Here is a V16 Auto-Union.

LEFT: *The Mercedes-Benz W125 of 1937 was the world's most powerful GP car; a record it held until the mid 1980s.*

BELOW: *The German teams also went record breaking: this was the specially streamlined 1938 V12 model.*

BOTTOM: *The 12-cylinder 1936 Mercedes-Benz record*

For 1968 it was called 'Sting Ray', but 'Stingray' took over thereafter. Coupe and convertible styles were available, with lines somewhat reminiscent of the latest Ferrari Supercars (and that is exactly the impression Chevrolet wanted to give). The chassis had disc brakes all round, and engines of up to 7 liters/427CID were on offer. The most powerful engines of all had 435hp, but as United States exhaust emission laws bit deeper and deeper the large and powerful options gradually faded away.

The fourth-generation model was built from the end of 1967 until the beginning of 1983, gradually losing its character and its performance, and gradually putting on weight, as legislation tightened around it. Compulsory '5mph' bumpers were skilfully blended into the style from 1973, a coupe body derivative followed for 1978, and front and rear aerodynamic spoilers were added for 1980. Yet sales increased up and up, with nearly 54,000 vehicles being built in the peak production year of 1979.

The sensationally beautiful fifth-generation Corvette arrived during 1983, with a completely new backbone chassis, suspension, steering and glassback body style. Except that the ride was bone-shatteringly hard in Gymkhana trim, the handling was sports car-like in every way — much better than that of any other American car. By this time the V8 engine was a 5.7 liter/350CID size, with 205hp (net), which still made it one of the fastest cars on American roads, for it had a top speed of 142mph, even though fuel consumption was usually about 18 miles per gallon.

This, however, was only the beginning. More powerful engines and a fully convertible body derivative were produced in the next two or three years. The Corvette was as popular as ever, still attracting red-blooded American motorists in large numbers. It will continue to do so for many more years.

OPPOSITE: *The latest, stunningly beautiful Corvette was put on sale in 1983.*

ABOVE: *The 1967-1983 Corvettes were built as convertibles or coupes, some with fastbacks and some with long noses . . .*

BELOW: *Mean machine, a 1984 example of the modern Corvette.*

LEFT INSET: *There were several different types of Ferrari 250GT, but the most famous of all was the race-proved short-wheelbase Berlinetta of the early 1960s.*

RIGHT INSET: *Until the early 1960s every Ferrari was a two-seater. Then, in 1960, the Pininfarina-styled 2×2 seat 250GTE was launched. Some 950 such cars were built.*

BELOW: *The first V8-engined Ferrari was the 308 family, introduced in 1973 and still selling today in 328 form. This is a 308GTB.*

SFG 728X

400hp. It was no wonder that most 250GTs could approach 150mph, while the Superfasts were good for more than 170mph. The most famous of this generation were the 250GT Berlinettas and the 250GTOs which followed them, for these were beautiful cars that also won many GT races.

As production increased, a series of 'standard', but still sensationally beautiful, body styles was developed, though many one-off bodies, especially convertibles, were still produced from time to time. Standard shapes were usually by Pininfarina, though Scaglietti of Modena generally made the shells to this design.

In the meantime, Ferrari came to prominence in Grand Prix and sports car racing, began winning in the early 1950s, and have been winning ever since. It was often said that Ferrari merely built road cars to help finance his racing in the early days. This was certainly true, but by the 1960s the road cars were in great demand on their own and the one side of Ferrari helped publicize the other.

Major design changes were made to the Ferrari line-up in the mid-1960s, not only when a new chassis with all-independent suspension and a rear-mounted drive train was produced for the 275GTB, but when a completely new type of smaller, transverse mid-engined 'Dino' was put on sale.

The 275GTB retained a front-mounted V12 engine, and was later replaced by 365GTB/4 Daytona, which could reach nearly 175mph and is often said to be the world's fastest-ever front-engined road car. At first the Dino was sold without

OPPOSITE ABOVE: *The 275GTB was revealed in 1964.*

OPPOSITE BELOW: *The 308GT4 of 1973 had a mid-mounted V8 engine,*

Bertone styling, and 2+2 seating.

BELOW: *This was the original mid-V6 Dino style of 1967-1973. Most had 2.4-liter engines.*

Ferrari badges, as a 'Dino' marque (the name was that of Ferrari's son, who died in his twenties), but every Ferrari enthusiast knows it as a Ferrari. Early cars had 2.0-liter V6 engines, but a 2.4-liter engine was later fitted.

From 1969, Fiat took financial control of Ferrari (and actually built a Ferrari-engined Fiat Dino of their own at this time), which allowed Enzo Ferrari to concentrate on his beloved racing cars. It also allowed Ferrari road car production to be increased. Ferrari built more than 1000 cars in a year for the first time (1246 in fact) in 1971, and this rose rapidly to 2221 in 1979. By the mid-1980s demand had increased still further and Ferrari production was exceeding 3000 a year.

To replace the V6 engined Dinos, Ferrari then introduced a series of mid-V8 engined models in the 308 (later 328) family. More sensationally still, to replace the Daytona, the mid-flat-12 engined Berlinetta Boxer went on sale in 1974; it was in its turn replaced, 10 years later, by the even more beautiful Testarossa. A few front-engined cars, latterly the 400 and 412 four-seaters, continued, but by the 1980s Ferrari was the world leader in fearsomely fast and beautiful engineered mid-engined two-seaters and 2+2.

In 40 years, Ferrari has probably produced more new, modified, or different engines than any other company, whether for road or racing cars. A study of the many Ferrari books shows engines as small as 1.0-liter, as large as 7.0-liters, in configurations as different as the famous V12s, V6s and V8s, plus flat 12s, flat eights, straight fours, straight sixes and even, on one occasion, a parallel twin.

No other company, not even Lamborghini or Porsche, has ever produced a car with the charisma of a Ferrari, which is every schoolboy's dream. You could drool over the styling, over the engine, or even over the noise, but best of all you can always drool over the name – Ferrari!

BELOW: *Perfect for California and Hawaii, if not for Europe — the open-topped 308GTS, complete with four-cam V8 engine.*

INSET RIGHT: *The superb 365GTB/4 Daytona, with 352hp and a top speed of around 175mph is probably the world's fastest front-engined road car.*

The Morgan Approach

So they do make them like they used to...

IN an old-fashioned factory at Malvern Link, Hereford and Worcester, today, new cars are still made to an old style. Every week, 10 or 11 new Morgan sports cars are delivered. Not only do they look and handle like a model of 50 years ago, but they are constructed in the fashion of that period as well. On the other hand, their performance – top speed and acceleration – is right up to modern standards. A Morgan, in other words, is a fascinating combination of progress and tradition. It is no wonder that one advertising slogan reads: 'The First and Last of the Real Sports Cars.'

HFS Morgan started in Malvern with a bus service, then moved into hire cars, considered building motor cycles, and finally launched the very first Morgan – a three-wheeler, with one (driven) rear wheel – in 1910. For the next 25 years this was the only type built for sale. However, even the original Morgan had independent front suspension, of sliding-pillar type, a feature which has been retained to this day. Then, as now, the factory was at Malvern Link; the firm moved into today's building in 1919.

If we assume that a 'car' has four wheels, then the first Morgan car was put on sale at the end of 1935, in a form that would still be recognizable and familiar to a Morgan buyer in the late 1980s. The separate chassis frame had Z-section side members, there was sliding-pillar independent front suspension, and a starkly styled sports car body shell, with steel panels fixed to a wood (ash) framework. The ride was bone-shattering hard, but the car had nimble handling and an enormous amount of character and verve. Early cars were fitted with 1122cc Coventry-Climax engines, with a Meadows transmission separated from the engine by an alloy tube that encased the drive shaft.

In the last half century, Morgan has firmly resisted all temptations to modernize the basic concept of this car, even though every component has been changed in one way or another. New engines and new drive trains have been phased in from time to time, the car's wheelbase and track dimensions have gradually increased, and there have been a few minor concessions to modern styling trends and safety requirements.

Two-seater tourer, four-seater tourer, and drop-head coupes have been offered at times, and for a short (and

RIGHT: *In 1950 Morgan announced the new Plus 4, complete with 2-liter Standard Vanguard engine. The sliding-pillar suspension is used on all Morgan cars.*

OPPOSITE BELOW: *The original four-wheel Morgan 4/4 style of 1936 has been retained, slightly modified, for more than 50 years.*

BELOW: *Morgan built three-wheelers for a quarter of a century before turning to cars. This is a 1934 Supersport, fitted with a water-cooled Matchless engine.*

137

Very Exclusive Cars

For very exclusive customers

NO matter how hard the economic climate, the rich will always be rich. If more of us knew why, perhaps more of us would be rich. Ah, well. . .

In automobile industry terms, this means that there will always be a sale, if only a restricted sale, for truly dignified and exclusive cars from Rolls-Royce, Bentley, Hispano-Suiza and Mercedes-Benz. Not Supercars, you understand, and not outrageously styled monstrosities, but cars for gentlemen and their families. It is a market, however, which is almost impossible to broach, unless there is a lot of tradition to back up that attempt.

By the 1930s, the four cars already named had sliced up the market between them as most other cars faded away. Pierce-Arrow and Marmon were killed off by the Depression and its after-effects. Bugatti was not in the business of building refined and practical road cars, Isotta-Fraschini was well past its best days, while Cadillac and Lincoln had both gone for quantity, instead of limited-production quality, sales.

RIGHT: *The Duesenberg J was introduced in 1928, and produced until the mid 1930s. The customer could specify any type of bodywork on the car's 200hp chassis – this Rollston-bodied Victoria was delivered in 1931.*

BELOW: *Duesenberg built the most powerful American car of the early 1930s – the 320hp supercharged eight-cylinder SJ model. This was so costly that only 36 cars were ever built.*

The British Daimler concern, though still building sleeve-valve engined cars, and continuing to supply the British royal family with its limousines, was also steadily moving down market.

Hispano-Suiza was the first to abandon automobile manufacture for 'top people', in 1938, after a glittering period between the wars. There were two outstanding Hispanos: the six-cylinder H6B model introduced in 1919, at the time the most advanced in the world, and the magnificent V12 model of 1931-38 which was faster, grander and more imposing than any other car of its day. Only if you had the pleasure of driving behind that splendid 9.4-liter engine, perhaps swathed in a Saoutchick, Binder, or Letourner et Marchand body shell, did you know for sure that no one else, king or tycoon, could surpass you on the day!

Even though Mercedes-Benz made more and more small-engined family cars in the 1930s-50s period, and had to recover from being obliterated by bombing in World War II, it still made a few truly remarkable top-of-the-range cars. In the 1930s there were two different types of Grosser model — both with supercharged straight eight-cylinder engines. The first was an old-fashioned car with hard springing, but the

1938-39 variety had an advanced chassis, gargantuan eight-seater body, and was mostly sold to Nazi leaders who found its impressive size to their liking.

The modern 'Grosser,' however, was the angularly styled 600 range introduced in 1963, which was even more technically advanced than the Rolls-Royce Silver Shadow with which it had to compete. You simply *had* to be a 'top person' to afford a car that had self-levelling suspension, power-operated everything, a 6.3-liter engine, and was so long and heavy that it helped to have acres of parking space wherever you stopped.

After Rolls-Royce bought up the bankrupt remains of Bentley in 1931 (some say, to kill off the excellent 8-liter, others so that they could take control of the famous Le Mans-winning marque's reputation), it really had the lion's share of all top-drawer car sales, a happy situation that the company has held to this day.

A new Bentley, based on Rolls-Royce components, was announced in 1933, and for the next two decades the Bentley was marketed as a sporting car ('The Silent Sports Car' was its advertising slogan), while the Rolls-Royce was marketed as 'The Best Car in the World.'

Until the mid-1960s, Rolls-Royce sold its products on the quality of engineering and construction, rather than on technical modernity. Only the short-lived Phantom III's V12 engine of 1935-39 was ahead of its notional rivals. Components such as servo-brakes (after Hispano-Suiza), synchromesh transmission (General Motors), coil-spring independent front suspension (Packard, in particular), and the V8 engine (Chrysler and Cadillac especially) were all seen on other cars before 'The Best Car. . .' adopted them.

The feature that really sold the Rolls-Royce and Bentley marques to wealthy customers was the quality, exclusivity and style of the coachwork. Until 1939, the cars were all supplied as rolling chassis to coachbuilders, who had taken the individual orders from the customers and built bodies to suit. Most of these had wooden framing and hand-beaten or rolled skin panels.

Rolls-Royce introduced factory-designed 'standard steel bodies' on Bentleys from 1946, and on Rolls-Royce Silver Dawns from 1949. However, all the post-war Phantoms (the very rare IV and the more numerous Vs and VIs) have special coachbuilt shells, as did the mouth-watering selection of Bentley Continentals built from 1952 on. Since the standard

In Europe in the 1930s, if you were truly rich — and discerning — you might buy a V12 Hispano-Suiza. Without doubt this car had the best chassis in the world, and the special bodies usually matched it. The stork mascot was quite unmistakeable to all lovers of fine cars.

cars retained separate chassis until 1965 it was quite usual to see special coachwork on these cars too.

From 1946 to 1965, the technical specification of Rolls-Royce cars gradually fell behind the times, for components like drum brakes were kept during that period. However, from 1966 the Silver Shadow models (and their Bentley T-Series equivalents) took over, combining typical Rolls-Royce quality and the usual patrician radiator style with a much lower monocoque shell, self-levelling suspension, disc brakes, full-power hydraulics, a V8 engine and automatic transmission.

It is a recipe that clearly appealed to the customer, for sales gradually increased to more than 3000 cars a year. There seems to be no likelihood of the 'Best Car in the World' losing its attraction in the next few years.

OPPOSITE INSET: *Every Mercedes-Benz Type 600 Grosser was large and impressive, but the really large examples were the long-wheelbase Pullmans, with six passenger doors.*

BELOW: *The British coachbuilder H J Mulliner got together with Bentley to produce the R-Type Continental in 1952. It was sleek, graceful – and very fast.*

Every military Jeep rode on knobbly tires, which whined unmistakably on surfaced roads, and the spare was bolted on to the tail. There was no space for baggage – you either carried stores or people (and sometimes both) in the rear seats. However, the Jeep was also expected to be able to tow a trailer, and many of them did.

From 1942, Jeeps were being used by the United States forces, by the British and by the Russians. Before the end of the war it was normal to find them carrying out tasks as various as distribution of mail behind the front line, scudding round the deck of aircraft carriers with bomb-carrying trailers behind, being used as radio vehicles, and even carrying light machine guns in the role of fast scout car. Top speeds were no more than 60mph, but with all that transmission noise, the whine of the tires, the bumping up and down on the seats, and the smells of the countryside coming straight in over the open sides, it felt like double that. No one drove a Jeep quietly and no one could be dignified in such a machine for long. It was a truly American concept and was as American as chewing-gum and baseball – and the Germans never developed anything quite like it.

By the end of the war, Willys-built or Ford-built Jeeps were almost indistinguishable, for both used the same engines, drive trains and basic structures. No fewer than 550,000 of original type were produced, so it was no wonder that they seemed to be everywhere, and used for everything. Perhaps a Jeep was not quite a consumable item, to be discarded at will, but many seemed to be abandoned if they broke down. In the American Army especially, there seemed to be a plentiful supply of jeeps in store which could be used to replace the 'empties' that had been cast aside.

After the war the Jeep design was gradually updated and civilized, so that it became the standard off-road leisure machine, as well as a valuable working tool, all over the world. It also inspired the birth of Britain's Land-Rover, Fiat's Campagnola and a host of other imitations.

TOP LEFT: *This CJ6 has huge non-standard tires.*

LEFT: *A 1979 Wagoneer, a more highly developed jeep for the private market.*

BELOW: *4+4 Jeeps can go almost anywhere – this Cherokee Chief is in the desert.*

OPPOSITE: *All dressed up, for use in the Philippines.*

pletely free hand. His view, quite simply, was that all the world's small cars without exception had wasted some passenger space because of styling, so he would concentrate all his efforts on improving this situation. The result was the ADO 15 project, which the world now knows as the Mini.

He decided to concentrate all the engine/drive train bulk in the same place, and to eliminate a front-to-rear drive shaft through the passenger compartment. This meant that he could mount the engine and drive train at the front, with front-wheel-drive, or at the rear, to drive the rear wheels. With weight distribution and ultimate roadholding in mind, he chose front-wheel-drive.

He also wanted to make the car as short as possible, while still being able to carry four full-sized adults. His stroke of genius, therefore, was to turn the engine sideways and mount it transversely, lift it slightly, and place the main transmission under it, in the sump. Instead of being at the front, the cooling radiator was to one side of the engine bay, drawing its air through holes in the left-side fender well.

Next he decided that as conventional-sized fender wells always intruded on passenger space, he would cut down the wheel size dramatically. The Mini became the first British car ever to use 10-inch diameter wheels. The suspension was also very compactly laid out, with trailing arms at the rear.

The result was that the whole package was squeezed into an overall length of 10 feet and a width of 4 feet 7½ inches, and the unladen weight was a mere 1340 pounds. However, because the 848cc engine produced 34hp, the Mini had a brisk performance and a top speed of nearly 75mph. Alec Issigonis gleefully claimed that, of the 10-foot length, at least 8 feet was allocated to passengers.

OPPOSITE: *Stark-bodied Mini Mokes have been built since 1964.*

OPPOSITE, INSET: *The privately-developed Mini Sprint had lowered lines and rectangular lamps.*

BELOW: *Many designers copied the Mini layout: here, a Fiat 127.*

However, not only was the Mini tiny, but it also had astonishing roadholding, handling and stability. The steering was inch-accurate, the small car could be threaded in and out of traffic in a very nimble fashion, and on twisty country roads it was as fast as much more expensive cars. It also had lashings of that elusive feature in a car, character, which endeared it to everyone who drove it.

Within months, every rival factory in Europe had bought a Mini, studied it and stripped it out, to see what they could learn. They learned a lot — and none of it was reassuring for companies wedded to the old style of designing cars. It was not just the Mini's amazing road manners or its irrepressible character which worried the opposition, but the breakthrough in packaging that Issigonis' team had achieved.

As it stood, there was a lot wrong with the Mini that ought never to have been copied, but there was also much that was right. The Mini's rubber suspension was too hard and too expensive to produce (whereas the Hydrolastic suspension that followed it in the mid-1960s was too queasily supple); there were really too many problems in asking a transmission to share its oil with the engine; the driving position was cramped; and the trunk was really far too small.

On the other hand, the amount of passenger space was incredibly generous for such a small car, and the behavior of the front-wheel-drive chassis was quite faultless. With a bit more money spent on quality control, a few more inches on length and width to improve accommodation still further, and maybe a hatchback to increase the stowage possibilities, and who knows what could be achieved?

Within three years Issigonis had extended the Mini formula with the more spacious 1100 models, and within five years the first rival cars were ready, starting with the Autobianchi Primula of 1964 and the Peugeot 204 of 1965. Once the Japanese chimed in, with cars like the little Honda N360, the trend was obvious to everyone. Nowadays, as a result of Alec Issigonis' bright ideas, front-wheel-drive and transverse engines are the norm for all compact car designs.

Unsafe at Any Speed?

The Corvair story

WHEN it was announced in the autumn of 1959, the Chevrolet Corvair caused a real stir in the world of the automobile. By the time independent testers had tried out the 1960 model its initial high reputation was already beginning to slide. After Ralph Nader's book *Unsafe at Any Speed* was published it became almost unsaleable. Yet the Corvair was neither as bad, nor as good, as was stated. What was it all about, and what went wrong?

The Corvair was conceived in the mid-1950s, at a time when all of Detroit's 'Big Three' — Ford, Chrysler and Chevrolet — turned to what became known as the compact car. Three new cars, one from each group, were launched in 1959; even though they were compacts, they were all six-seaters. The difference, however, was that Ford and Chrysler designed conventional front-engine/rear-drive cars, whereas Chevrolet produced a very way-out machine indeed. It was not coincidence that the ugly but reliable VW Beetle was at the height of its reputation in the United States, or that the General Motors line was currently very staid and in need of a shake-up.

Led by its adventurous chief engineer, Ed Cole, the Chevrolet design team not only conceived a sporty compact car, but one that aped many things that had worked so well for VW. The new model, which was eventually given the name 'Corvair', was completely different from any previous Chevrolet — and different, indeed, from any previous American car.

Like the VW Beetle, the Corvair was given an air-cooled engine, mounted at the rear, along with both independent front and rear suspension. Because of the restrictions on available space, the back end was a simple swing-axle design, and more than half of the car's weight was over those rear wheels.

Unlike the Beetle, however, the Corvair was given a 2.3-liter flat six engine, in 80hp or 95hp tune; allegedly this was inspired by Ed Cole's interest in light aircraft. Unlike the Beetle it was offered with a choice of three-speed or four-speed manual transmission, or with two-speed automatic transmission. Its kerb-side weight was about 2400 pounds, creditable by other General Motors' cars' standards, but at least 100 pounds more (all at the back end) than Ed Cole had hoped.

The other major technical innovation was that it was the very first Chevrolet to have a unit-construction body/chassis design, this being engineered around an easily recognizable body style, with what became known as a 'bathtub' ridge around the waistline. In the current fashion then prevailing in the United States, it had four circular headlamps. Two-door or four-door sedans and a four-door station wagon were all offered on the same chassis. Incidentally, it was a triumph of packaging that a rear-mounted engine and rear-loading station wagon body could both be found on the same car; even VW was impressed.

At first it was sold as the 700 Series (cheap), or 500 Series (very cheap), though in 1960 a more upmarket version, the 900 Monza, came along with bucket seats and a two-door coupe style.

The Corvair's problem was that it handled like no American car had ever handled before. All other current models understeered, whereas the Corvair felt much more 'nervous' and oversteered. It needed much lower front than rear tire pressures even to feel safe, and there was always the possibility that the tail would try to overtake the front in hard cornering or wet road maneuvering. Very few run-of-the-mill American drivers could cope with this — nor many journalist testers. It was not until 1962 that Chevrolet offered a stiffer handling package, and not until 1964 that a transverse compensating spring was fitted to help cut down rear-wheel tuck-under.

ABOVE: *Chevrolet's Corvair was completely different from every other American car. Its engine was in the tail, and was an air-cooled flat-six.*

RIGHT: *The Corvair had all-independent suspension, and 'bath-tub' styling.*

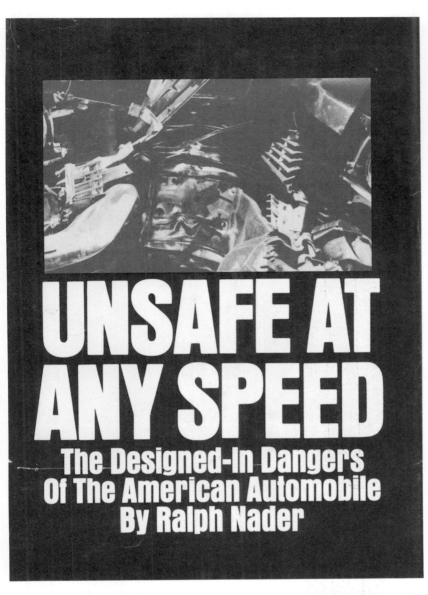

UNSAFE AT ANY SPEED
The Designed-In Dangers Of The American Automobile By Ralph Nader

Even though there was criticism of the Corvair's handling and of the quality of its construction, Chevrolet went out for the sports-car market in the next few years. Monzas eclipsed the sedans, while the station wagons sold only slowly. More powerful engines came along, as did a convertible called the Monza Spider, and GM even became world-leaders by introducing a turbocharged engine option on the most upmarket version.

Enter Ralph Nader, a young crusader trained in the law, who took up consumer matters, with automobile safety as his speciality. By 1964 he had homed in on General Motors' overall attitude to safety, and in particular their lack of progress with the Corvair. His celebrated book, *Unsafe at Any Speed*, put the skids under a car that was already well past its peak, and not even the launch of a radically improved Corvair for 1965 could stem the tide.

The 1965 Corvair had much better chassis, with wishbone rear suspension, and there was a Corsa model with 140 or 180hp which took over from the Monza Spider. In 180hp form this Corvair could reach 115mph and run with the best of British sports cars. Not only that, but there was a smooth new body style, with a more flowing fender line, and altogether better trimmed interiors.

It was a great car, but it was all too late. The GM Board had already taken the decision to let the Corvair project wind itself down, so the 209,000 cars in 1965 slumped to 86,000 in 1966, and to a mere 12,887 in 1968. About 1.5 million Corvairs had been sold before the directors had clashed with Ralph Nader in open court proceedings, and just 125,000 thereafter. In May 1969 they announced that Ed Cole's dream car was to be killed off, and there was no 1970 model.

It would be a long time before General Motors was so adventurous again.

Wankel's Engine

Whatever happened to the rotary engine?

I
F the Man from Mars landed on earth tomorrow, no doubt he would be amused by the archaic engines used on most of the world's cars. For aircraft, ships and many types of railway locomotive, power is provided by pure rotary engines. But for cars there are the crudities of converting reciprocating piston movements into the rotary movement of a crankshaft. Clearly, he would say, these Earthlings have got it all wrong — if pure rotary power works for their large transport machines, why not for cars?

Perhaps if Otto's reciprocating engine had not been the first to develop, and had not worked tolerably well right from the start, it might never had made it to the first centenary of

ABOVE RIGHT: *Dr Felix Wankel poses proudly behind an early example of the famous rotary engine which bears his name. The rotor tip seals which caused so many problems are clearly visible.*

RIGHT: *The first Wankel-engined car to be put on sale was the NSU Spider of 1964, which had a single-rotor engine mounted in the tail.*

OPPOSITE ABOVE: *This was the book which effectively killed off the Corvair, and did great harm to GM's corporate image. Even so, the late-model Corvairs were fine-handling machines.*

OPPOSITE: *Here is another GM Corvair project car of 1964, the Monza, again never put on sale. Its easy to see where the mid-engined Corvette styles of the late 1960s came from.*

the automobile. Perhaps it is only habit that keeps the world building car engines this way? Or is it?

Until gas-turbine aero-engines were invented in the 1930s, and brought into military and commercial service in the 1950s, there was no alternative – though man the inventor often tried to find a better way. Surely there *had* to be a better way?

Dr Felix Wankel (like his illustrious predecessors, Otto and Diesel, also a German-born engineer) thought he had the answer. Like most of his peers he realized that scaling down the dimensions of gas-turbine engines was always going to be incredibly difficult and expensive, so he set about designing a different type of rotary.

The Wankel engine, as it became known, used the idea of a specially shaped rotor revolving inside a chamber of even more specialized shape; the rotor needed an eccentric shaft (a crankshaft, really) to give it the appropriate movement. In that way, a fuel/air mixture could be sucked in, compressed, exploded, and expelled from the annular spaces formed between rotor and chamber, therefore producing power. It was not pure rotary power, but it was a start.

The original engines of the 1950s were single-rotor units, which felt unbalanced and suffered from all manner of problems. Yet NSU, of West Germany, were interested, worked together with Wankel, and eventually put the world's first Wankel-engined car, the two-seat Wankel Spider, on sale in 1964. It was a pretty little car, with the engine mounted in the tail, and from a (nominal) 500cc engine which produced 50hp, it had a top speed of around 90mph.

The problem for NSU was twofold. To make such engines in volume, an entirely new generation of precision machine tools had to be designed, financed and installed. To make the engines reliable, a mountain of work was needed on the tip that separated the rotors from the chambers.

The pundits, and in small numbers the public, were impressed, so NSU took a deep breath and went to the next stage. In 1967 it launched the futuristic Ro80 sedan model,

OPPOSITE: *In 1969 Mercedes-Benz announced the triple-rotor C-111 research project.*

OPPOSITE, INSET: *The Wankel-powered C-111 had its engine behind the seats, and used gull-wing doors.*

ABOVE: *The NSU Wankel Spider, was the first Wankel-powered car.*

BELOW: *The NSU Ro80 of 1967 had a twin-rotor engine.*

in which there was a 105hp *twin*-rotor Wankel engine. This gave the car sports sedan performance, was smoother and quieter than the original, seemed capable of unlimited engine revs, and was a very attractive proposition.

Except that it was still very unreliable, and very expensive to build. All over Europe, Ro80 engines blew up after 10-20,000 miles of high-speed life and cost a fortune to be replaced. NSU struggled on with development, balanced its costs as well as it could, but eventually had to merge with VW. It was the beginning of the end for this branch of the Wankel engine.

In the meantime, Wankel development was breaking out all around the world. In West Germany Daimler-Benz started testing, as did Rolls-Royce in Britain, while Citroën came to a coproduction agreement with NSU. In the United States, not only Curtiss-Wright (who built aero-engines), but General Motors took out licenses, while in Japan it was Toyo Kogyo (whose cars were sold with Mazda badges) which took up the challenge.

Wankel fever was at its height at the end of the 1960s. Not only had Mercedes-Benz shown the impressive triple-rotor C111 mid-engined project car, which looked, and was, as fast as any racing sports car in the world, but Mazda's first Wankel-engined car, the 110S Cosmo coupe, had been put on sale, closely followed by several others. The mighty General

Motors announced that its own Wankel-engined cars would be launched on the market by 1974.

Unhappily for Wankel himself, the big breakthrough never came. Costs of engines, and cars fitted with them, remained high, and the bad publicity of premature failure could not be hidden. The public became suspicious when firms like Rolls-Royce and Mercedes-Benz tested and tested, but never brought themselves to put Wankel-engined products on sale.

When compared directly with their rivals, it was found that Wankel engines were not as fuel-efficient, and engineers also discovered that it was very difficult for a Wankel engine to meet the increasingly severe exhaust emission laws which the world's legislators were pushing through and for this latter reason it was dropped by GM and Ford. Only Mazda persevered, for by 1973 they had four such cars – R100, RX2, RX3 and RX4 – on the market.

Then, in 1973-74, the bottom dropped out of the market. Israel clashed with Egypt in the Middle East, the Organization of Petroleum Exporting Countries (OPEC) dramatically pushed up the price of crude oil, and the days of cheap gasoline supplies were over for ever. Mazda's sales of rotary-engined cars plunged and General Motors abandoned their production program. NSU phased out the Ro80, and every other research program was slashed.

In the end, only Mazda stayed the course. It made dramatic improvements in reliability, fuel-efficiency and the level of exhaust emissions, and announced the fast and attractive Wankel-engined RX7 coupe in 1978, of which eventually hundreds of thousands were sold. A new generation of RX7s took over in 1986, but it is still the only Wankel-engined production car in the modern world. Will it ever have a rival?

Throughout the 1970s Mazda persisted with the Wankel engine, and sold hundreds of thousands of RX7 sports coupes. The second-generation RX7 Savanna was launched in 1985, has 185hp, and a fast 140mph maximum speed.

Ten Million Cars Each Year

Detroit's great post-war expansion

BRITAIN'S automobile industry stopped car production almost as soon as Britain declared war on Germany in September 1939. But Detroit, in an America still at peace, carried on building cars full blast until the beginning of 1942. The production lines then turned over to making weapons of war as diverse as the Jeep and the Sherman tank, Rolls-Royce Merlin aero-engines and six-wheel-drive trucks. Nevertheless, when victory over Japan was finally achieved in August 1945, the private-car assembly lines had been closed down for less than four years.

In North America, as in Europe, there was a huge pent-up demand for private cars when the war was over. Not only had a lot of older models been worn out or crashed in the intervening four years, but the release of millions of self-confident military veterans into civilian life at that time also meant that there was a great deal of money washing around in the United States.

Although it took time for Detroit to produce new post-war models, the wait was worthwhile. One of the most startling early-1950s styles came from Studebaker, courtesy of the Loewy studios.

As in Europe, most of the early post-war American cars were pre-war designs. Some had been introduced as recently as 1941, but some were considerably older than that. No matter – the tools and facilities were dug out of store, refurbished and set into action again. Anything, it seemed would sell. From 1945 to 1948, the best-selling Chevrolets were modified 1942 models. So were the Fords, and so were the Plymouths.

Most of the car-makers recovered rapidly from their military efforts and began building cars again during the autumn of 1945. Seventeen marques – with Ford and Chevrolet at the pinnacle and Crosley at the bottom – closed down in 1942, and the same 17 reopened for business in 1945. It looked like business-as-usual; if you had slept for four years you would have noticed no change.

But then, for 1946, two new marque names entered the fray: Frazer and Kaiser. These cars were the twin brainchilds, logically enough, of Joe Frazer and Henry J Kaiser, the first already renowned in the automobile industry, the other a ship-building tycoon. They took over the redundant Ford bomber aircraft assembly plant at Willow Run, near Detroit, and set out to challenge the Detroit 'establishment' at its own game. Also, Tucker said it was going to build lots of sleek new cars, but the project died at birth.

That, in fact, was the last upheaval in the *status quo*, for the established United States automobile industry had shrugged off these latecomers by 1955. It also quietly killed off several marques of its own in the decade which followed, though others were launched in their place.

In the last pre-war year, the Americans had produced 3,760,000 private cars, with General Motors right on top of the heap, taking a 48 per cent market share, Chrysler behind them with 23.4 per cent, and Ford third with 18.3 per cent.

LEFT: *Throughout the post-war expansion. Cadillac had Detroit's best-equipped and best selling luxury range of cars. All the cars had powerful V8 engines, this being a 1953 Coupe de Ville model.*

BELOW: *Madison Avenue's advertising genius at its best – this is a promotional still for a late-1950s Cadillac.*

RIGHT: *Cadillacs looked better in some years than others. This 1952 example had a very dumpy roof line, but that didn't stop the US citizen queueing up to buy.*

ABOVE: *In the mid 1960s Chevrolet was America's best selling car and the Impala its most familiar range. This was a 1964 Convertible, one of nearly 900,000 Impalas built in that year. Prices started at about $3,000.*

LEFT: *Ford's Mustang, launched in April 1964, appealed so much to young buyers that the first million were sold in less than two years. The best way to go cruisin' was to have a convertible, like this 1966 example.*

RIGHT: *The Pontiac Firebird (this is a Trans Am) was developed by GM to fight the Ford Mustang. All used the same formula — four seats, open or closed bodies, and hundreds of options.*

much that, for the first time, the United States had to start importing oil from abroad. The balance of power – literally, for crude oil was liquid power waiting to be refined – had shifted in favor of the Arab states.

When gasoline was cheap and plentiful, car-makers did not worry too much about fuel-efficiency or weight savings. Every year, it seemed, cars got larger, heavier, more powerful and more thirsty. In America, for instance, it was normal for a car to have more than 300hp, to weigh more than 4000 pounds and to achieve little more than 10 miles per gallon.

In the meantime, the Arabs had come to own more than half of the world's known oil reserves. They also set up the Organization of Petroleum Exporting Countries (OPEC) in an attempt to square up to the oil barons, and to control –

and if possible increase – their selling prices. By 1973, when crude prices had already been pushed up by a few cents a gallon (because of the United States' dominance, prices were always quoted in American currency), it looked as if there was less then 20 years' supply still in the ground.

OPEC was already flexing its muscles, ready to impose a large price rise, when the October 1973 war broke out. OPEC then also decided to use oil as a political weapon. Countries deemed to have helped Israel were denied supplies for a time, while all others suddenly had to pay no less than four times as much for their oil as they had previously done. The impact of this pressure was enormous – and there was no way around it. Other oil producers, recognizing a good profit when it was offered, also raised their prices to suit.

RIGHT: *Soaring oil prices led to the development of new small-car diesel engines. VW's small four-cylinder unit, used successfully in the Golf, set new trends right across Europe.*

BELOW: *In 1971, a Cadillac Brougham like this was ideal for North American conditions, but by 1974 it suddenly looked heavy and thirsty.*

Cleaning Up Exhausts

The impossible takes a little time

IF it had not been for the peculiar climatic conditions of the Los Angeles basin, there might have been no serious control of car engine exhaust systems until the 1970s. However, by the 1960s, as North America's most motorized city, Los Angeles began to suffer from serious smog problems. The cause, as researchers later confirmed, was the conversion of many different emissions into a foul-smelling fog. But the automobile got most of the blame.

When the car was first invented in the 1880s, it was enough of a miracle that an explosion of a gasoline/air mix- ture could be harnessed to produce power, and no thought was given to what was in the exhaust gases. For some years, in any case, there were so few cars, producing so little power, that their exhausts did not present a problem. The odors emitted by the automobile's rival, the horse, and the deposits left behind in its passing, were equally noxious.

Once cars began to dominate city streets, and the phrase 'traffic jam' became known, exhaust pollution became a problem. Quite simply, the burning of gasoline with air pro- duced several exhaust gases. The least harmful of these was steam, but the obnoxious compounds included oxides of nitrogen, carbon monoxide (which is potentially lethal, if breathed in sufficient concentration), and unburned hydro- carbons. These all had objectionable smells, could harm plant life, and were suspected to be harmful to people and animals who breathed them.

They were doubly dangerous because they were invisible. The smoke from a diesel engine, especially when it was cold, was obvious, and of course it tasted awful and left a deposit, but it was no more harmful, and you could tell it was there.

By the 1960s, the pollution problem was becoming serious in many cities, though not at all noticeable in the country- side. The Los Angeles problem was made worse by what is known as photochemical reaction, where the hot Californian sunshine interacted with the nitrogen and hydrocarbon compounds to form a brown fog. The fact that electric power stations and aircraft all added to the chemical soup went largely unmentioned. The automobile was marked out as the prime culprit.

The first legal steps to control, and eventually to reduce dramatically, the emissions from car engines, were made in the United States. In the early 1960s all engines had to have closed-circuit crankcase breathing (where oil fumes were fed back into the inlet manifolds), but by the late 1960s legisla- tion required all the emissions to be drastically reduced. Stringent high-mileage endurance tests had to be carried out by all car-makers to prove that their engines would not lose their tune as they grew old.

LEFT: *To cut down on pollution and to protect the environment unleaded fuel was introduced into the USA in the 1970s and Europe in the 1980s.*

BELOW: *Getting the last pollutants out of car exhausts was difficult and expensive, and could only be achieved by using exhaust catalysts.*

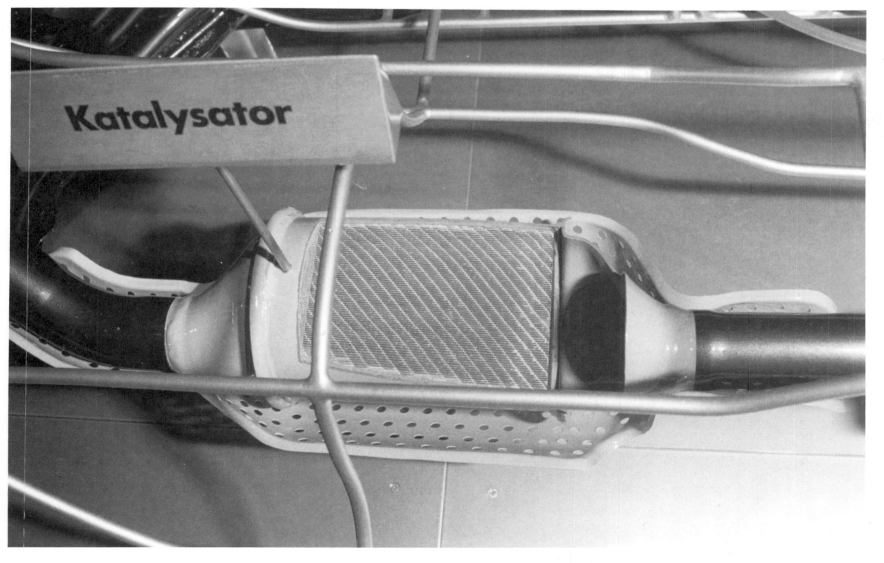

RIGHT: *Jaguar's new XJ6 took six years to develop, and went on sale in 1986 to widespread critical acclaim. The specification is packed with advanced electronics, the car more refined than any of its ancestors.*

BELOW: *The Ferrari Testarossa has a 390hp flat-12 engine mounted behind the seats, a five-speed gearbox, all-independent suspension, and a 180mph top speed. A peerless super car for the late 1980s.*

OPPOSITE ABOVE:*Sports cars like this 1936-style Jaguar SS100 looked magnificent but had awful aerodynamics. The front encouraged lift and to reach 100mph was something of a miracle.*

OPPOSITE: *Although many people hated the looks of the mid 1930s Chrysler and De Soto Airflow models, it was a praiseworthy attempt to smooth a car's lines to reduce the drag and improve performance and fuel economy.*

ABOVE: *When Mercedes-Benz produced the W196 sports car for racing in 1955, the aerodynamics were carefully considered. Headlamps were faired in, exhaust pipes were sited in a 'dead' area, and for Le Mans there was a moveable air brake mounted behind the cockpit.*

There are great difficulties to be solved:

Brakes get too hot if they do not get enough air to cool them – but too much air causes drag.

An engine cooling radiator needs lots of air to keep temperatures in check; too much causes drag, too little causes overheating.

A smooth underside lowers drag, but may encourage the engine, drive train and exhaust system to overheat.

The ideal shape for aerodynamics may be wrong for the running gear – and the people – to be fitted inside.

The ideal shape for straight-line speed may be very unstable in a side-wind.

The stability may change as the speed rises, due to a change in the position of what is known as the 'center of pressure.'

The body shape might begin to generate lift as speeds rise, in just the same way as an aircraft wing lifts the airplane off the runway.

RIGHT INSET: *Although based on the 911's layout, the 959 was a limited-production competition car with four-wheel-drive, and water-cooled cylinder heads.*

LEFT INSET: *By the mid-1980s the basic 911 had been turbocharged, given a new nose, extra engine air inlets, and looked just like a road-going race car.*

BELOW: *Originally designed for VW, this became the 924, Porsche's best-selling car of the 1970s and 1980s. For 1986 it had a Porsche engine, and was called the 924S.*

Downsizing the Monsters

Facing up to economic reality in the USA

TWENTY years ago, the roads of North America were full of enormous cars. But not any more. Since then, American cars have been shrinking, and the change is not yet complete. The vast old-style cars are now described as 'dinosaurs,' and although a few very large cars are still being made, the day of the North American 'land-cruiser' has gone for good.

How and why did this happen? In summary: after World War II American cars continued to grow as the nation's prosperity increased and the price of raw materials and gasoline stayed low. The downturn came in the 1970s, and more obviously in the 1980s, as costs rose rapidly and gasoline needed to be conserved.

In the 1950s and 1960s there never seemed to be a need to make American cars as compact as possible. There was plenty of road space, thousands of miles of new highways to use, and a great deal of money to be spent. Large, powerful, heavy and thirsty V8 engines, backed by automatic transmissions, were normal. Every time a model was changed or facelifted, it seemed to get a bit longer, a bit wider, with more weight balanced by more power.

As an example, in 1950 the best-selling Chevrolet Skyline had a 92hp six-cylinder engine and weighed about 3100 pounds. In the 1960 the Bel Air had 135hp, with V8 options up to 335hp, and weighed 3500 pounds. In 1970 Bel Airs and Impalas had V8 engines going up to 390hp and weighed about 3650 pounds. The same growth had occurred in every other American range of cars.

Detroit's bosses kept trying to stem the tide, but with little success. Usually they produced new lines of smaller cars, while allowing the existing cars to continue. Then the process started again, and the smaller cars got bigger, heavier and more powerful.

In 1959 there was a rush of new 'compacts' (Corvair, Falcon, Valiant), which soon led to 'super compacts' and 'intermediates' being produced. Then in the 1960s there was the relatively small-sized 'pony' car (Mustang, Camaro, Firebird), which also began to grow and to put on weight. General Motors and Ford usually led the way, with Chrysler and American Motors struggling to stay in touch.

In 1970 and 1971 the 'Big Two' tried again, with Ford announcing the 103-inch wheelbase Maverick, and then the tiny 94.2-inch wheelbase Pinto, while Chevrolet produced the 97-inch wheelbase Vega. That was just a sighting shot, for the need to 'downsize' was still a question of social responsibility rather than economic reality. Chrysler missed out, but American Motors cropped off one of their larger cars to produce the stubby Gremlin.

In the early 1970s, however, those economic pressures arrived with a vengeance. The fight to control pollution, conservation and rocketing oil prices (with the possibility of shortages in future years) led to reams of new legislation. Quite suddenly, vast cars were seen as wasteful and antisocial.

OPPOSITE ABOVE: *In 1960 Ford's Falcon was a 'compact,' which grew inexorably larger over the years. Ford later added the Maverick and Pinto lines to fill the gaps.*

OPPOSITE BELOW: *By the mid-1970s even the so-called 'personal' cars were very large indeed. These are the front-drive Cadillac Eldorados which weighed 5100lb.*

RIGHT, TOP TO BOTTOM: *A sequence showing the way the Pontiac Bonneville has shrunk over the years. The largest car was the new 1974 model, followed by the 'downsized' 1977 variety, the even smaller, squared-up 1982 version and finally the latest 1987 Bonneville. Weights have fallen from 4400lb in 1974 to 3300 in 1987.*

217

ABOVE: *A perfect example of a good car grown too large. This 1975 Cadillac Eldorado was 600lb heavier than the Eldorado of 1967, had a 6-inch longer wheelbase, and a 500ci rather than a 429ci V8 engine.*

LEFT: *For 1978, Plymouth took a bold step by introducing this European-designed Horizon as its base car. It had front-wheel-drive, a 105ci engine, and weighed only 2150lb.*

Market leader General Motors led the way and the rest made haste to follow. Even before the 1973/74 energy crisis erupted, GM had decided to downsize their cars, but it took three years to turn this plan into reality. The B-Body and C-Body models (cars like the full-size Chevrolets and the Oldsmobile Deltas) lost several inches in the wheelbase and up to 800 pounds in weight. In the years that followed, other ranges shrank too.

In the meantime, even smaller cars were 'taken over' from European and Japanese associate companies and sold in the United States. Ford began selling pint-sized front-drive Fiestas in 1977, while General Motors started building Chevrolet Chevettes in 1976. Chrysler produced the Plymouth Horizon (really a Chrysler/Simca Horizon) in 1978, while American Motors (AMC) added the grotesque Pacer to their model line-up.

At that time, the way to make cars smaller was to cut back on front and back overhangs, slim down the doors, and sometimes (without actually admitting it) make the passenger cabins a bit smaller. The next important step, first embraced by GM, was to give priority to passengers, and make engines and drive trains more compact.

The best way to do this was to adopt front-wheel-drive with transverse engines. The first GM cars in this style were the Chevrolet Citations of 1979, with four-cylinder or V6 engines. Ford, however, went one better, with a front-wheel-drive Escort of 1980, which was effectively an Americanized version of the new European Escort.

In the meantime, new United States legislation meant that all cars would have to get smaller – a lot smaller. New laws requiring a progressively higher Corporate Average Fuel Economy (CAFE) figure specified *average* fuel consumption figures of 21.6 (Imperial) miles per gallon by 1977, and no less than 33 (Imperial) miles per gallon by 1985. Failure to meet this would result in huge fines.

Marques like Rolls-Royce, which imported about 1000 cars a year, could afford to shrug off the new laws, but no American company could ignore them. It was obvious that the only answer, once again, was to make the cars progressively smaller, with smaller engines, and with higher fuel efficiency.

Everyone – managers, engineers and pundits alike – agreed that this eventually meant European-sized cars with front-wheel-drive were needed, and this is precisely what America got. General Motors decided to set up cooperative projects with the Japanese (several of their small mid-1980s

219

Let's All Hold Hands

The industry merges its resources

ARE you surprised to learn that some modern Volvos use VW or Renault engines? That a car called a Pontiac Le Mans is really an Opel Kadett built in Korea? That a Rover Sterling shares most of its engine, drive train and body structure with the Honda Legend? That the same basic structure went into the design of the Saab 9000, the Lancia Thema and the Fiat Croma?

If you did not know, do not be ashamed to admit it. The world's automobile industry is now a very complex business, for almost every company has links with another – commercially, financially or technically. Few of them would be able to survive unless they did.

BELOW: *Rover (Sterling) 800 and Honda Legend cars have different styling; top of the line cars share the same Honda engine.*

RIGHT: *The Rover 800 Series (Sterling in the USA) was a joint project between Austin-Rover in England and Japan's Honda.*

ABOVE: *Saab's 9000 uses its own unique type of 16-valve twin-cam engine, but has the same basic front-wheel-drive layout as the Lancia Thema and Fiat Croma models. The most powerful version has a 175hp output.*

LEFT: *The Lancia Thema of 1984 was the first of the jointly-conceived European 'Type 4' cars to be shown. It used Fiat engines, and had more in common with the Croma than the 9000.*

RIGHT: *The Fiat Croma was the third of the Type 4 cars to be launched, shares features with the Lancia and was to be joined by the other Type 4, the Alfa Romeo 164, in 1987.*

There is nothing new about mergers or the use of common parts. The world's biggest car corporation, General Motors, set the standard for everyone when it came into existence in 1908; famous names which joined together at that time included Cadillac, Chevrolet, Buick and Oldsmobile.

Even before World War II, other companies were getting together, trading their independence for security. Daimler joined with Benz in 1926, Morris took over Wolseley in 1926, Daimler annexed Lanchester in 1931, and before 1939 General Motors had bought up Vauxhall in England and Opel in Germany. Detroit's 'Big Three' corporations even began buying components from each other.

Until the 1960s, the 'urge to merge' was usually due to tycoons wanting to get bigger and more powerful; entire companies got together and individual identities were lost. In recent years there has been a much more basic reason. It has now become so expensive to design, and tool up for, new engines, drive trains and models, that few companies can

afford to do it on their own; nowadays they tackle joint design projects and share in the results, but otherwise stay aloof from one another.

Until the 1960s, cars were relatively simple. Car-makers either built their own products or bought them in from specialist suppliers. It was usual for them to build their own running gear, but quite a number went outside for bodies, or perhaps for specialist drive trains.

At this time, though, they began to learn from General Motors and Ford. Not only did these massive combines make sure that engines and drive trains were shared between makes and models, but sometimes even between countries. By the beginning of the 1970s, General Motors' Australian Holden cars had a lot in common with European Vauxhalls or Opels, Ford were building essentially the same cars in Britain and West Germany, while both had satellite plants assembling similar cars in South Africa and South America. Soon after this they forged financial links with Japanese

concerns – GM with Isuzu and Ford with Toyo Kogyo (who made Mazdas).

Then came the energy crisis, the rapid increase in gasoline prices and the worldwide inflation that followed. At the same time cars were becoming more complex and had to meet many more sets of regulations. Large corporations could cope with this, but the smaller 'independents' found it difficult to obtain the money for modifications and new models.

During the 1970s, therefore, almost every car-maker talked to every other one, desperately looking for ways to merge ideas without merging their business, looking for novelties which they could afford, and looking for ways to bring down costs.

The large corporations themselves, with worldwide interests, began to edge their way towards the 'world car.' General Motors' T-Car project – an Opel Kadett in West Germany, a Vauxhall Chevette in England, a Chevrolet Chevette in the United States, an Isuzu Gemini in Japan, and a different type of Chevrolet Chevette in Brazil – was a perfect example. Ford, for their part, introduced a front-drive Escort in Europe, and a similar but not identical Escort in the United States.

The independent companies did it differently. They soon found that they were happy to swap engines and drive trains – 'building blocks,' as they became known in automobile-industry jargon – while jealously guarding their individual body styles.

The 'arm's-length' link-up between Peugeot and Renault of France and Volvo of Sweden was typical. Each company wanted a new large-capacity engine, but none could find the resources to do this alone. By getting together and agreeing to share the investment, they were able to solve the problem. The PRV V6 engine was announced in 1974; it then found its way into several new cars in the next few years, and is still in production today. It even appeared in the ill-fated De Lorean sports car.

In Europe, in particular, things began to get very complicated. Ford of West Germany supplied engines to Saab. Volvo bought six-cylinder diesel engines from VW. Porsche bought automatic transmissions from Mercedes-Benz. British Leyland bought manual transmissions from VW. Fiat began a new small-car engine project with Peugeot (which was later cancelled). Renault provided small four-cylinder engines to Volvo-Holland.

RIGHT: *Although this 1985 car is called a Chevrolet Nova, it was derived from the Toyota Corolla, using Toyota engines and transmissions. Other modern Chevrolets are Suzuki and Isuzu based.*

OPPOSITE: *Austin-Rover's Maestro, announced in 1983, used VW manual and automatic transmissions.*

BELOW: *The smart French Renault 25 uses the same four-cylinder engines as Citroën and Peugeot and the same V6 engines as Peugeot and Volvo.*

Then the true joint projects came to the surface. The pan-European 'Type 4' project began on the basis of a common floor pan and suspensions for new Saab, Fiat and Lancia models; before long the similarities decreased, but Alfa Romeo joined in as well. British Leyland joined forces with Honda to produce the Ballade in Britain as the Triumph Acclaim; the next-generation Ballade was named Rover 200, but the result was the same. Alfa Romeo got together with Nissan to produce the ARNA model (Alfasud engine/drive train in a Nissan Cherry structure). More such schemes will surely surface soon.

In North America, the process is well advanced. The 1986 Chevrolet line started with a Sprint that was a modified Suzuki, the ancient Chevette, the Spectrum that was a modified Isuzu, and a Nova that was a modified Toyota. American Motors' Renault Alliance and Encore were modified Renault 9s and 11s.

The miracle is that companies like BMW and Mercedes-Benz are still independent.

BELOW: *Renault linked with AMC to produce the Alliance (USA) and the Renault 9 (France).*   RIGHT: *The Mazda 323 of 1980 was similar to the new front-drive Ford Escort.*

New Fuels for the Future

Is there another way?

ABOVE: *Electric cars have never been successful, though they have always been around. This was a fairly early example of this type, an Arrol-Johnston of 1913.*

OVERLEAF: *For a time the steam-powered Stanley was popular – this is a 1911 model – but the last cars were produced in 1927; essentially an interesting oddity.*

PERHAPS it is significant that the automobile was not invented until there was a suitable fuel – gasoline – to drive it. Automobiles have now been around for more than 100 years, and gasoline is still the best power source to drive them. Millions of hours – and a great deal of money – have gone into research for alternative fuels, but nothing practical has yet been discovered.

The problem is that gasoline (and diesel fuel) usually has to be refined from crude oil, and this is one of the world's limited natural resources. It took hundreds of thousands of years for oil to be created under the earth's surface, the supply is not inexhaustible, and it now looks as if all easily recoverable sources will have been used up sometime in the twenty-first century. There were times in the 1960s and 1970s when Doomsday seemed much closer than that, and the search for an alternative intensified.

But what to use instead of petrol? Not diesel fuel, which comes from the same source. Steam power? Electrical energy? Solar power? Fuel cells? Atomic power? Alchemy (the 'pill into water equals gasoline' trick)? Or the still-to-be-discovered 'wonder material?'

Steam, electricity, solar power and fuel cells can all provide power, but none of them gives cost-effective energy. In short, they are not practical. Gasoline and diesel fuels offer a formidable number of advantages, which any alternative has to beat. They are compact (an enormous amount of energy is locked inside a small volume of material), cost-effective for

the customer, cheap to extract, easy to transport and safe in operation. At the moment, nothing else can match them.

From time to time, of course, publicity-conscious inventors claim to have produced new fuels, or to be able to turn water into gasoline by adding small quantities of a magic preparation. This makes wonderful headlines for the newspapers – until the inventors are asked to prove their claims. In every case, this challenge has been declined.

Credulous people suggest that such inventors are 'bought off' by the oil companies, to kill the opposition to oil and therefore preserve the monopoly, but this has never happened in reality. Chemically, of course, there is no way to transmute water (which contains no hydrocarbons, and specifically no carbon) into a combustible fuel by adding any material.

Although cars have, indeed, been powered by steam or by electricity, they have never been economical to run or practical machines. Steam cars are silent and pollution-free, but the steam has to be produced by generating heat. The best way to produce this heat is by burning oil or gas, so the world's ecology gains nothing, especially as there is a loss of heat efficiency in the process.

Time and time again, electric cars have been built, tested and abandoned. Time and time again the designers have found that a huge bulk – both mass and weight – of storage batteries is needed to produce even the sluggish perfor-

ABOVE: *In the early days it took time for design trends to settle. Not only was this 1899 Hautier cab powered by electricity, but the driver sat at the rear!*

OPPOSITE ABOVE: *The T4 of 1961, the last of Rover's gas turbine car experiments.*

OPPOSITE: *A 1980s fashion was to develop 'hybrid' machines, sometimes driven by petrol engines and at other times by electric power. Like this Fiat, none progressed beyond the experimental stage.*

mance of a town car. Batteries need to be recharged every night, and this can only be done by plugging into the mains. Electricity is supplied from power stations. Most stations get their power by the burning of coal or oil, but this is not as cost-effective as burning petrol *in situ*, on the car itself.

There is, of course, a third power source, nuclear fuel, but this is not at all acceptable to the world's environmentalists.

If it was possible to produce electrically powered cars with smaller, more compact and more efficient batteries, this might become an acceptable alternative. For generations, however, the electrical industry has been striving to perfect an alternative to the lead-acid accumulator, but without success. If a driver was willing to pay spacecraft prices for his power supply, his needs could be satisfied, but this is not likely to happen.

Britain's most prestigious department store is the Harrods emporium in London. For many years all Harrods goods were delivered in the capital by electrically powered vans like this. If such vehicles could be given a better performance and greater endurance they would be a viable proposition for a wide variety of uses.

Acknowledgements
The publisher would like to thank
Design 23 who designed this
book, Melanie Earnshaw who did
the picture research and Pat
Coward who compiled the index.
We would also like to thank the
following agencies, institutions
and individuals for supplying
illustrations on the pages noted:
Audi-Volkswagen: pages 93 (both),
    95 (inset), 96 (top), 173 (both),
    187 (inset)
Autocar: pages 14 (top), 15, 25
    (below), 122, 141, 148 (top), 161
    (top), 166 (main), 167, 191,
    203, 228, 234 (top)
Autocar/Nick Walsh: pages 198-
    199
Autosport: pages 148 (below), 165
    (main)
BBC Hulton Picture Library: pages
    9 (top), 10 (below), 11, 17
    (below), 20, 21 (below), 24
    (below), 44 (below), 52 (top), 55,
    56, 57, 65 (top), 73 (top), 81
    (top), 98 (top), 185 (both), 229
Henry Austin Clark Jr: pages 18
    (both), 21 (top), 25 (top), 26
    (below), 27 (both), 30 (top), 33
    (below), 35, 48 (below), 52
    (below), 59 (below), 60 (both),
    62-63 (main picture), 75 (top),
    79 (below), 83 (inset), 112
    (below)
Classic and Sportscar: pages
    28-29, 34,58, 84, 85 (below),
    115 (inset), 117 (top), 126
    (main), 174 (main), 180 (top)
Classic and Sportscar/Nick
    Baldwin: page 40 (below)
John Colley/Haymarket
    Publishing: page 111 (top)
C W Editorial: Pages 1, 6, 29
    (below), 31, 40 (top), 50 (below),
    67 (below + left), 76 (top),
    82-83, 89 (top), 90 (top), 99,
    119 (below), 138-139, 140, 150
    (inset), 164, 165 (inset), 175
    (below), 207 (inset), 210, 211
    (top), 213, 214-215
Esso Petroleum: page 190
Fiat Auto (UK): page 125 (below)
Ford Motor Co: pages 51, 79 (top),
    86 (top), 144 (top), 181 (below),
    193 (below), 197 (inset), 206-
    207, 234 (below), 235 (below)
General Motors Corp: pages 80,
    220 (inset)
General Motors Corp/Pontiac
    Motor Division: pages 105, 217
    (all 4)
G N Georgano: pages 50 (top), 75
    (below), 85 (top), 87, 89, 153,
    204-205, 218-219, 226
William F Harrah Automobile
    Museum: pages 2-3, 22, 23
    (top), 24 (top), 37, 39 (both), 47
    (top), 48 (top), 59 (top), 86
    (below), 137, 160
Harrods: pages 236-237
Haymarket Motoring Picture
    Library: pages 74 (top), 111
    (below & top), 112 (top), 145,
    147 (below), 162 (middle), 166,
    174 (inset), 175 (top), 228

(below), 233 (top)
Haynes Publishing: page 110, 204
    (top), 205 (top), 214 (inset)
Imperial War Museum: page 95
    (inset)
Jaguar: pages 152-153, 199
    (inset)
Mike Key: page 180 (bottom)
Land Rover Group: page 161
    (below)
Ludvigsen Library: pages 68-69,
    98 (2 below), 117 (below), 168,
    169, 170-171, 170 (inset), 171
    (inset), 172, 178-179, 184
    (below) 186-187, 200 (top), 201
The Mansell Collection: pages 8, 9
    (below), 10 (top), 12 (both), 13
    (below), 232
Mercedes-Benz: pages 13 (below),
    14 (below), 16, 17 (top), 64, 66
    (below), 67 (top)
Morgan Motor Co: page 136
Andrew Morland: pages 19 (top),
    33 (top), 47 (below), 53 (below),
    65 (below), 66 (top), 76 (below),
    77 (below), 88 (below), 96
    (below), 107 (top), 109 (top),
    121 (below), 123 (top), 129, 131
    (inset), 132 (both), 133, 134-
    135, 135 (inset), 138 (inset),
    162 (top + bottom), 163, 179
    (inset)
National Motor Museum Beaulieu:
    pages 156-157, 158 (inset), 183
Nissan UK: page 120
Porsche Cars Great Britain: page
    125 (top), 208-209
Porsche Cars West Germany:
    pages 126 (inset), 127 (both)
Quadrant Picture Library, Sutton,
    Surrey, SM2 5AS: pages 19
    (below), 26 (top), 28 (below), 30
    (below), 32, 36 (top), 39, 41, 53
    (top), 61, 63 (inset), 70 71, 72,
    73 (below), 74 (below), 81
    (below), 88 (top), 91 (below), 97,
    100 (both), 108, 109 (below),
    111 (middle), 121 (top), 124,
    125 (below), 137 (top), 149, 176,
    182 (below), 188-189, 193 (top),
    194, 195, 196-197, 200 (below),
    212, 215 (inset), 218 (below),
    220-221, 224, 225 (top), 235 (top)
Road and Track: pages 46, 184
    (top), 188 (inset), 230-231
Rolls-Royce Motor Cars: page 78
Richard Spiegelman: pages 36
    (below), 54, 77 (top), 78 (below),
    103 (inset), 104 (both), 106
    (top), 106-107, 142-143, 143
    (inset), 144 (below), 177, 178
    (inset), 182 (top), 202 (both)
TPS/CLI: pages 102-103, 116
    (below), 146, 147 (top), 150-
    151, 158-159
TPS/Keystone: page 128
TPS/Three Lions: pages 23
    (below), 101, 192
Toyota: page 123
US National Archives: page 45
Vauxhall Motors: page 43 (top)
What Car: pages 222, 223, 227
    (below)
Nicky Wright/National Motor
    Museum Beaulieu: pages 154-
    155, 155 (inset)